TAKING NOTE O

Third Way Books

All You Love is Need (Tony Walter)

What's Right with Feminism (Elaine Storkey)

The Steeple's Shadow (David Lyon)

Taking Note of Music (William Edgar)

Transforming Economics (Alan Storkey)

THIRD · WAY · BOOKS

TAKING NOTE
OF MUSIC

William Edgar

First published in Great Britain 1986
SPCK
Holy Trinity Church
Marylebone Road
London NW1 4DU

British Library Cataloguing in Publication Data

Edgar, William
    Taking note of music. — (Third way books)
    1. Music—Religious aspects—
Christianity
    I. Title   II. Series
    261.5′7   BR115.M/

ISBN 0-281-04255-1

Typeset by Pioneer, Perthshire
Printed in Great Britain by
Whitstable Litho Ltd, Whitstable, Kent

To Barbara,
my covenant companion

Acknowledgements

Unless otherwise stated, the Scripture quotations in this publication are from the Revised Standard Version of the Bible, copyrighted 1946, 1952, © 1971, 1973 by the Division of Christian Education of the National Council of the Churches of Christ in the USA, and are used by permission.

The extract from 'Quatuor pour la Fin du Temps' by Olivier Messiaen is reproduced by permission of Durand S.A., Editions Musicales, Paris/UMP © 1945.

The extract from 'Quartet for Strings, No. 4', Opus 37 by Arnold Schönberg is reproduced by permission of G. Schirmer Ltd.

The extract from 'Wiese im Park' (*Four Songs*, Opus 13, No. 1) by Anton von Webern is reproduced by permission of Universal Edition AG Vienna (Alfred A. Kalmus Ltd).

The extract from 'Waltz for Debby' by Bill Evans is copyright © 1962 Kensington Music Ltd and Acorn Music Corporation, and is reproduced by permission.

The extract from 'Nervous Waltz' by Erroll Garner is reproduced by permission of Octave Music Publishing Corp.

Contents

Preface   xi

Introduction   1

1   A World of Music   3
2   Jubal's Bequest   22
3   How Does Music Mean?   52
4   Spiritual Forces in Music   79
5   Making Melody to the Lord   101

Notes   134
Index   143

THIRD WAY BOOKS
Series Editor: Tim Dean

Third Way Books aim to explore the relation between biblical Christian faith and political, social and cultural life. SPCK and *Third Way* magazine have joined together to publish a series that will introduce some contemporary writing to a wide audience.

Third Way is an evangelical magazine which seeks to provide a biblical perspective on politics, social ethics and cultural affairs. Further details from: *Third Way*, 37 Elm Road, New Malden, Surrey KT3 3HB.

Preface

In some ways this book is a team effort. Although I have been working on the problem of a Christian view of music for over twenty years, I have had lots of help. It has been something like a multiple treasure-hunt, if there is such a thing. In following through on different notions I have had opportunity to test them against the views of musicologists, composers, aestheticians and friends. When conclusions have been reached it is difficult to trace them back to their source. Thus in one sense it is impossible to give credit where credit is due.

Nevertheless a few names stand out where the link is quite evident. I first want to thank Tim Dean for his proposal to write the book, and for his encouragements all along. He and the publishers have been very patient. Several other people played important roles in the early stages, and I would like especially to mention Evy Anderson, Harold O. J. Brown, Edmund Clowney, Victoria Hobson and Mary Ann Wynter. Thanks should go as well to the FOCUS Study Center, and to my parents, for providing an ideal setting for me to work on the manuscript. I am grateful to the Columbia University Music Library for allowing me to be guest scholar there for several weeks.

I have a special debt of thanks to my three readers, Adrienne Chaplin, Alan Davies and David Porter, whose many competent suggestions were often incorporated into the text. Knowing the time commitment this involves, I appreciate their help all the more. Finally, I am more than grateful to my family, whose understanding and encouragement during the birth-process of the present volume were remarkable.

Aix-en-Provence, March 1986   *William Edgar*

Introduction

Over the last few decades Evangelical Christians have been increasingly concerned to explore the relationship between their faith and the arts. A few books on aesthetics have appeared, some of them very helpful indeed. Yet to my knowledge very little exists in the specific area of music. Other than a few histories of hymnody, and an occasional guide for church musicians, there is nothing much on the problems of musical aesthetics.

In recent years I have been involved in discussions and study groups in which the participants have raised many of these questions with great insistence. Many of them revolve around the same issues: Can Christians make music in the secular world with a good conscience? What styles are appropriate? Is rock and roll manipulative? Does music have a message? What does the Bible teach us?

This book is about the nature and place of music in the modern world. Its aim is to explore some of the problems involved, and to come up with a few answers. Most of us do not think about music objectively. We either pay no particular attention to aesthetic questions, and simply give way to what is happening, or else we nurture our likes and dislikes, our favourite traditions, and leave criticism to those who seem to care. It is my hope to provoke deeper, more objective thinking about the area of music, because I am convinced that the stakes are high, and the issues too important merely to leave alone.

Although some of the material in the study may give the impression of being kaleidoscopic, there is a certain logic behind the different steps taken. First, we shall need to consider the pervasiveness of music in our world, and some of the ways it affects our lives. We will find that there is much to rejoice in. But we will also see that not all is beneficial. After this, we shall look at the teaching on music to be found in the Christian perspective. Specifically, we shall consider a number of facets of the Bible's presentation of music and the arts. The idea is not to bring in some

1

'religious jaw', nor is it to reduce the issues to 'sacred music', whatever that may be. Rather, it is my deep conviction that the basic framework within which we can work out some of the problems we face in the world of music is that of biblical truth. Not that the Bible is such an easy book to understand when it comes to the arts. But a careful look at its basic message will allow us to gain some ground in accomplishing the purpose of this study.

Perhaps it would be helpful to state this purpose at the outset, as I am not certain whether the opportunity will arise in the ensuing material to state my goal in so many words. The overall purpose of this book, then, is to describe the nature and richness of music as a function of the Creation. Both the enjoyment and the responsibility in music should be rooted in the will of God, and this is determined by looking at what he has revealed. It is my hope that this preliminary study will encourage us to regain the world in the area of musical activity, which is one part of life in the Kingdom of God.

This is not a Christian manual for good composition. Although some of the principles suggested apply to the problems of composition, the appeal of the book is meant to be broader. The intended audience includes not only the musician but also anyone who is generally concerned about aesthetic questions in relation to spiritual matters. Neither is this meant to be an introduction to music history from a theological point of view. Such a book needs to be written, but the present study is more modest.

1: A World of Music

'Cleo, give me some Egyptian moves.' This order is directed to a reclining figure on a barge decorated with hieroglyphics. A slave-master directs four 'galley-slaves' who are pushing the boat toward the shore to the beat of a drum. In another section of the craft a toga-clad Julius Caesar stands, smiling at the Queen of the Nile. Cleopatra then removes a pair of sunglasses and begins to lip-synch the words to 'My New Boyfriend'.

Video-clips have established themselves firmly in the music market. They are rapidly becoming the only way to publish a hit song. The scene described above occurred on Menemsha Pond, Martha's Vineyard Island, Massachusetts. The famous singer Carly Simon was creating one more imaginative, rather bizarre clip in the hopes of succeeding in the very competitive popular music world. She hired one of the best directors in the business, Jeff Stein, who draws a yearly salary in the six-figure bracket. He regularly exceeds the budgets assigned to him because he knows profits will far outstrip the small losses. Stein works closely with Tony Mitchell, one of the most respected lighting and photography persons in rock video. With this talent, the pond can be made to look like the Nile in Egypt, and almost any illusion can be created. With tongue-in-cheek sequences these sound-images can combine the Hollywood scenery of an epic movie with the lyrics of a modern song, all carefully programmed to appeal to a mass audience.

Television stations all over the world carry these clips, giving this new art-form the largest exposure that any has enjoyed. Why is this so? How can it be that the medium of film has become one of the most important carriers of music in our century? Of course there are precedents, like opera, which combines music and drama. Music is often combined with dance and ritual. But clips are a strange modern equivalent of opera or dance. Instead of live musicians, we have dubbed sound. Instead of a stage, the small screen.

Video-clips could claim a more direct ancestry in some of

3

the ideas of the pioneers of modern dance. Dissociated imagery, spliced-in, cut-up sequences have a precedent in the modernistic choreographical techniques of Merce Cunningham. In his concept of the dance, he pioneered such things as the multiple messages of a fragmented, 'non-linear' programme well before rock clips were in vogue.[1] Life and art relate very directly, he believes, because life itself is not ordered in a logical way.

Is this true? Surprisingly, the presence of video-clips in our world—and we are bombarded by them in every possible place, in boutiques, bars, living rooms and restaurants—raises fundamental questions about art and life, questions that beg for an answer if we are to know how to handle the bombardment. And they concern far more people than Merce Cunningham was able to reach. What qualifies as music? Do the arts have boundaries between them? Does art itself have limits? Are there any moral criteria involved in our use of music, in our evaluation of it? What effect does music have on our psyche, on our behaviour?

What is new is not the fact that music serves another medium, say, film. Music has often undergirded other functions besides its own. One does not usually attend a ballet, or church, for the music alone, however important its role may be. In fact, if the music in ballet or in worship is not authentic, we will be disappointed. What seems new is that music has become a consumer product, to be taken in without much thought. We hear it, because it is there, but it does not demand anything of us. The question could be asked, whether such music could stand on its own. The problem is not a brand new one, but it presents itself in our century with insistence, partly because it has had to vie with other media. The film director D. W. Griffith once exclaimed, 'If I ever kill anyone it won't be an actor but a musician.' He had been arguing with his collaborator in *The Birth of a Nation*, Joseph Carl Breil, about the musical score for the film. They planned to insert a Wagner piece, and Griffith wanted to change some of the notes to fit the images better. But Breil was outraged at the idea of tampering with Wagner. Griffith retorted that, being for motion pictures, 'it wasn't primarily music'.

Since that time composers for film write their music with the visual sequences in mind, carefully synchronizing sound

4

and image, in order to enhance the viewer's awareness. They may do it 'literally', using tense sounds to back up suspense or soft ones for romance. Or they may do it through less direct relationships. Unless there is a memorable theme song, however, few people are interested in listening to the sound track alone. Now, this may be all right in the case of films, since their primary purpose is not the musical experience. But what happens in the case of video-clips, which do intend to sell a song? Can the music stand on its own? Or does it need to?

Sound and Silence

The availability of music in the modern world is astounding. Our fathers would have stood in wonder had they confronted our modern means of reproducing sound. It is hard for us to imagine, but their world did not rejoice in records, tapes, radios and earphones. We sometimes forget our privilege. We can listen to Beethoven or Brahms performed under the world's greatest conductors, at an amazingly modest price, with a small cassette. Think how much the appreciation of jazz music would be hindered if we did not have access to the great musicians of the past, like Louis Armstrong and Duke Ellington. As it is, we can hear 'live' sessions without living in Harlem or Storyville.

Another advantage of the modern media is the availability of so many different kinds of music, wherever you are. Recently I was walking by the large student dormitory near the place where I work, and I could hear through an open window the exotic sounds of Arabic music. I thought to myself, how comforting for some Moroccan or Algerian student, far from his homeland, to be able to enjoy familiar sounds from his own culture, right in the midst of otherwise impersonal and confusing surroundings.

While some may lament the individualism promoted by the personal cassette player or walkman, we must admit that there are times when it is marvellous to be able to 'tune out' the noisy world, and find solace in the beauty of recorded sounds. The additional advantage of these personal earphones is that we don't have to contend as much with the intrusive portable radios.

The positive sides of the availability of music today are

many. However, we cannot overlook some of the problems raised by the 'omnipresence' of sound and the sound media. One rarely attends a concert where one is not disturbed either by clicking cassette-recorders, flashing cameras, or people rushing around to adjust and fiddle with knobs and wires. We cannot help but feel that there is a kind of imperialism of recording and filming devices, to the extent that scaffolding and wires spoil the atmosphere of many concert halls.

A more serious kind of intrusion, ironically, is by the music itself. A friend of mine, a renowned violinist, was eating at a restaurant after a performance. The inevitable background music was piped in. He asked the waitress if it might be turned off. He politely explained that he was a musician, and that there were times where he needed silence. He further explained, in the simplest terms he could find, that this particular music bothered him because it lacked real structure and had no real interest. The waitress simply answered that other customers did not seem to be disturbed, and that the music was just there, not to be noticed, and that, in short, my friend had no right to impose his view on all the others. It was an unsettling dialogue, because we witnessed the musician, in this case a very great one, asking for silence instead of the mindless sounds being reproduced, arguing with the non-musician who was deciding in favour of it, not on aesthetic grounds, but because it was part of the décor and not to be tampered with!

People from various cultures in various periods have, of course, listened to music while they ate. But in a sense the performance had 'boundaries', it was 'over there', beyond the table. One could applaud the performers after each piece, admire their instruments, smile at them, and even dismiss them at the appropriate time. The same is no longer true. Like the video-clips we discussed above, background music also has interesting antecedents. Rollo Myers, Erik Satie's biographer, informs us that during the intermission of a play by Max Jacob, early in this century, an innovation was tried out. There would be 'furnishing music' in the halls and stairways. It was played live, of course, but the audience was specifically told to disregard it, and consider it as part of the furniture. Monotonous sequences, fragments from larger well-known pieces, were played over and over. In a way the experiment was a failure, because people were so intrigued by the presence of instrumentalists outside the concert hall that they listened intently. They were amused by the whole idea, rather than passively letting it by. But within a few generations music would indeed become part of the furniture, and people would ignore the presence of the sounds that are subtly invading them. Today music is just *there*, like the air we breathe.[2]

True silence is now a rare commodity. It is proper to speak of noise pollution. Even in remote places, out in the country, we are followed around by sounds produced by men. Not that total silence is desirable either. There are many advantages in having music accompany the activities of our lives, at work, in leisure, worship, social gatherings. But there are danger points as well. Most of them are aesthetic. But some are physical. According to recent reports there are at least one hundred million people (within the area of the twenty-four-nation Organization for Economic Co-operation) who live or work near places where they are regularly exposed to noise-levels above sixty decibels. An accurate measure can be established which correlates a number of health hazards to high decibel levels. High blood pressure is one of them. Hearing impediment is another. Younger generations will have losses of auditory perception because they regularly subject themselves to high volumes.

The noise factor is only one small aspect of the problem. The aesthetic questions are also extremely important. The two are related, as well, because a number of musicians seriously propose to redefine music so it can include all sound. In 1913, for example, with characteristic optimism, the composer Luigi Russolo defended 'l'art des bruits' (the art of noises) with the passion of an ideological liberationist. As a visionary he rejected the past, with its 'accursed silence', and heralded the coming of 'noise-sound', a necessary by-product of the machine age, a welcome freedom from the bondage of convention. Thus Russolo advocated that we take infinitely more pleasure in the sound of a tramway, of a car, or of a screaming crowd, than in those of Beethoven's *Eroica* or *Pastoral Symphony*.[3] More recently such ideas have been tempered and refined. A whole new medium has been developed since the 1950s, using electronics in various

7

combinations with natural sounds. Probably the best-known modern exponent of electronic music is Karlheinz Stockhausen. Much of his music is based on the idea that the distinctions between 'natural', 'human', and 'synthesized' sounds are not clear, nor should they be. Inspired in part by an Oriental way of thinking, Stockhausen believes that all distinctions in the world can be exaggerated, and that in fact they should be minimized. He is fond of saying that there is no black or white, but only shades of grey. In his music, he tries to implement these theories. For example, *Mikrophonie 1*, composed in 1964, uses microphones as the principal instruments. Sounds are generated from a tam-tam activated by glass, metal, wood, rubber and synthetic materials. Hand-held directional microphones are linked up to an electric filter, which in turn is connected to an amplifier and speakers. All of it is then recorded on to a tape, improvising on the filters and other controls for variation.

Synthesizers and electro-acoustical devices are now common fare in the music world. The widest range of sounds imaginable can be produced. The electric guitar is becoming old-fashioned, as we see the rock band taking on voice processors, electric drums, and keyboard synthesizers of all sorts. Again, the question is, where are the boundaries? How fast can we gallop into the brave new world of electronics before the omnipresence of sound becomes a serious problem? French composer Pierre Henry goes so far as to use human brain-waves as an instrument. In his *Corticalart*, written in the early 1970s, he attaches wires to the head and improvises on the amplified sounds of the brain impulses. He, like Stockhausen, tends to believe that all is in all, and that anything can be interchanged with anything else, in the name of creativity.

We live indeed in a world of sound. Some of these sounds are difficult to evaluate. The multiplicity of sound-phenomena is confusing and even threatening. Yet their presence is insistent, and their challenge can hardly be ignored. As a first step, let us try to sort out the issues involved by examining four musical challenges coming out of this modern world of music. This will be a preliminary look at four questions which our musical culture impresses on us, before going on to the central considerations of the following chapters.

The Kingdom and the Power

'Is it not strange that sheeps' guts should hale souls out of men's bodies?' Young Benedick's aside in *Much Ado About Nothing* takes on even greater significance in a world where music saturates every corner. On 14 July 1985 about 1.5 billion people in more than a hundred countries heard the same concert. The 'Live Aid' rock festival was broadcast from London and Philadelphia, by satellite, to every place on earth. The goal of the extravaganza was to raise money for victims of famine in Africa. The performers were the 'superstars' of rock music, people like Paul McCartney, Mick Jagger, Elton John, Bob Dylan, David Bowie and Eric Clapton. The power wielded by this largest concert ever is quite staggering. Not only in terms of the money raised, but also the amazing feat of having such a diverse group of musicians work together testifies to the power of the event.

It can be safely said that if it were not for the media, neither the tragedy of the famine nor the resources available to help out would have been current knowledge. As such we can only be glad for what happened. Just the same, certain difficulties emerge. Compassion-at-a-distance is always somewhat risky. People are more likely to be impressed with the media event than truly concerned for the complex problems of Ethiopia which produced the famine. And many will nurture their illusion that anything is possible through music. Those who watched the concert closely could not help but notice that at least one of the performers, Bob Dylan, was ill at ease. That his heart was not in it completely was later confirmed in a rare television interview, where he flatly stated his objection to the theme song 'We Are the World', because, said he, man is not able to save himself.

The means, moral philosophers would remind us, do not always justify the ends. If the power of music to do good is multiplied because of the technical means at our disposal, it is not always clear what that good is. The abundance of music, its omnipresence, is a factor of power which we need to reckon with if we want to avoid seduction. Music has become a luxury, in the literal sense of the word, whose root meaning is 'over-abundance'. The humblest modern man can do what no king of antiquity could manage: enjoy music from any period, in any style, at any volume, just by the twist

9

of a few dials. The wealthiest potentate of the past could not assemble even a small musical ensemble for an evening's entertainment without an elaborate hiring process, scheduling problems and financial preoccupations.

If modern people have it so much easier, they also have a problem not really present for the ancients. They must decide what to listen to. So much is available, what do they choose? That is the question! But the answer depends on one's view of the power of music. While almost everyone recognizes that music has some influence on us, the consensus ends there. Some believe that music can indeed manipulate us, and induce behaviour-changes in us whether we try to resist or not. Others disagree. To them music has little more effect on us than a meal, or a change of weather.

Whatever our view, we must first recognize that this is an important issue. It is certainly one that is taken seriously in Eastern countries. A number of governments have been firmly convinced of music's power to inculcate ideology in their citizens. But they are not always consistent in applying a certain view to their policies. It would have been convenient, for example, to be able to point out the kinds of musical manipulations practised by the Stalinist regime in the 1930s, and to contrast that with the relative freedom enjoyed in the West. But things are not so simple. In fact, we lack solid studies on music in the Soviet Union that could help us understand the aesthetics of a modern totalitarian state. Volkov's recently published *Memoirs of Dmitri Shostakovich* cannot be trusted, as it turns out under the scrutiny of careful examination.[4] In them the great composer tells of his supreme professional sacrifices in order to live at peace with the bureaucratic view: his music had to be 'trivial' in order to please. But it happens that much of this sensational material had been previously published in the USSR, probably by a malcontent. Just the same, there is evidence that Shostakovich had indeed co-operated with the government, and toward the end of his life was anxious to live that reputation down. He spoke of heavy burdens on his soul, of exhaustion and irritation because of the compromises he felt he had to make.

The truth is that the bureaucracy has not always been able to have things as it wishes. It may indeed have tried to shape popular musical taste, just as it was able to shape literary taste, with the success of realism. But even in Stalin's heyday, 'all transitions and changes are endlessly complicated . . . Overnight the system rushes to co-opt the very forms of popular culture which only yesterday it had vehemently resisted.'[5] What irony, that at the height of Stalinist repression, the most bourgeois values seem to appear in the arts, values that the spirit of revolution had been meant to exterminate once and for all. This tells us two things. First, how difficult it is to establish in a clear way the nature of music's influence on thought and behaviour. Second, it tells us that the arts are perceived to have a most important role, nonetheless, in shaping ideals. After the 'Great Proletarian Revolution' of 1966 Chairman Mao decreed that both flower gardens and music with a beat were unlawful. He promoted instead revolutionary operas such as *The Red Lantern*, in which all of the components were designed to inspire total allegiance to socialism.

We tend to scoff at such primal aesthetics. But is it true that democratic countries are free from the imposition of norms? Western societies often have their own unwritten laws concerning art. The free market (whether it 'sells') is such a powerful factor in art that one wonders if there is not a capitalistic equivalent to the centralized state. In a consumer economy, the market becomes the final arbiter of aesthetic standards. The issues are not simple. It cannot be said to be altogether wrong, given the fact of an industrialized society, that the market should play such a strong role. Growing urbanism, increased dependence on technology, and the 'massification' of society brought with them certain needs. For various reasons, too complicated to go into here, religion failed to meet the deepest needs. So a moral and aesthetic vacuum was created, one which the arts seemed suited to fill. But they had to fill it on a scale suitable to mass society. It is not surprising, then, that with increasing industrialization and increasing technology came the means of providing music on a massive scale. With the growth of modern society in the late nineteenth century came sheet music, the gramophone record, public concerts, marching bands, and a tremendous growth in the musical instrument industry. Naturally the style of music changed as well. Among other things it had to suit the needs of millions of people with virtually no musical

11

background. To put it schematically, music became simpler, more accessible.

As such this is perfectly acceptable. Yet increasing the dissemination of music means increasing the means of manipulating it. In the right hands, this is of great value. But the opposite possibility is real. It is not easy to measure the power of music over people. However, many people count on it as being an undisputed fact that it does have a power. The Bulletin Company in America is the owner of the well-known service, 'Muzak'. They provide background music for offices, restaurants, airports and stores. The sound is usually fairly uniform, and the passer-by is unaware of its structure, but the creators of the particular musical texture used know exactly what they are doing. The composers and editors have learned which kinds of combinations produce desired effects. A recent advertisement reads: 'Muzak motivates people — keeps your morning bright all day long.' This odd sentence is followed by an explanatory statement: 'Music by Muzak is psychologically selected, arranged, recorded and programmed to vary throughout the day and fit the employee efficiency curve.' The accompanying picture shows two men joyfully sweeping the floor and dusting the wall. This is quite a claim. Is it less ambitious than the *Red Lantern* opera? Music has always accompanied work, and presumably it has helped people to get through the tasks. But do we want piped-in sounds to do this in a deliberate manner?

French Minister of Culture Jack Lang recently touched off a spark of controversy when he publicly suggested that the American television series *Dallas* was guilty of 'financial and intellectual imperialism'. It is true that one encounters the soap opera all over the world. It is also the case that the moral values encountered in it are often materialistic. Furthermore, the serial is easily available, because the international market for such a product is so well established. But is it really 'intellectual imperialism'? A similar accusation is launched against rock and roll music. A number of parents' organizations, alarmed at the number of off-colour rock songs flooding the market, are demanding that record companies affix an 'X' label to certain albums in which pornography or occultism are propounded. Many believe that children are being lured into degenerate behaviour patterns because of

12

this kind of suggestion in music. These questions cannot leave us indifferent. What is the power of music?

Production and Reproduction

This brings us to a second consideration. Music in the modern world is very dependent on the electronic media, as we have seen. Over ninety per cent of the music we listen to is delivered through loudspeakers, whether they are in plain view, hidden in a car dashboard, or inserted directly into the ear. On the one hand, this has incomparable advantages. School teachers can play examples to their classes, musicians can have access to different pieces for analysis, and we can hear the latest themes without going to a public concert. When we remember that J. S. Bach went blind because he spent hours copying musical scores by candle-light, before even playing them to hear what they sounded like, we can be grateful for our easy access to good music.

But with the privilege comes a responsibility as well. Ironically the great availability of different styles, and the ability of electronics to expand sounds in an almost infinite number of ways, may tempt us away from acquiring personal skills and disciplines. When results can come without blood, sweat and tears, there may be a price to pay. Jazz pianist Oscar Peterson was asked in an interview to reflect on the future of jazz. He expressed alarm at the small number of pianists capable of doing rich improvisation today, compared to the time when they could be found in every night-spot in the big cities. A major reason, according to Peterson, is that so many keyboards now are electronically equipped to deliver any sound, any beat, in any key, that the younger musicians simply do not bother to practise their scales and arpeggios for hours on end, as they used to. Hundreds of method books proclaim 'ten easy steps to jazz piano' or 'harmony made simple' so that simplicity is indeed replacing art. In a word, music is being *re*produced today more than it is being produced.

Thus performer and listener tend to operate at a certain distance from the 'raw material' of music. Morally, this in itself is neither right nor wrong. However, we are so used to hearing music filtered through the media that we sometimes forget the more natural sound. Several years ago, at the Nice

13

jazz festival in France, the Count Basie Orchestra was playing. As usual, it was well amplified, each instrument playing through its own microphone. At one point during the concert a circuit was broken. The lights went off, and so did the amplifiers. But the orchestra kept on playing, and for a few precious minutes the audience heard something quite extraordinary: the pure, natural sound of the Basie Orchestra. There was a bit of imbalance, but the timbres were rich, and the contrast between the brass, the reeds and the rhythm section was striking. When the current came back on, the audience was actually disappointed!

This anecdote hardly 'proves' that modern amplification is exaggerated. Fidelity control is a worthy art-form in its own right. But the fact of being at a distance from the natural sounds of the acoustical instruments means it should be handled with great care. Another delicate problem related to this is that because of the near perfection of recording techniques, performances heard over the media are 'perfect'. Every rough spot can be smoothed over, thanks to multi-track recording devices. This makes it very difficult, psychologically, for aspiring young musicians to listen to recordings without feeling they will never make it. This stands in contrast to older recordings, where flaws, pitch problems and mistakes were allowed to creep in. The story is told that when the great pianist Artur Schnabel finished his monumental recordings of the complete Beethoven sonatas, the studio engineer came to him and explained that there had been a number of mistakes here and there. If Schnabel would come down to the studio he could play over those measures and they could be dubbed in. Schnabel refused the offer. He even offered to do the entire thirty-two sonatas again, incorporating whatever new mistakes might be involved! But under no circumstances would he allow the studio to spoil the unity of the original performance, with the mood and ambience he had created.

The problem of reproduced music is part of a larger problem in our world of electronic media. Parents and school teachers have noticed the increasing passivity in children. Television can offer very rich programmes, and is an extraordinary tool for learning. But much of that learning is passive in nature. In the absence of 'live' teachers, or actors,

14

and of interaction with the subjects presented, there is not much else to do but absorb what is being put forth. Of course it is possible to discuss programmes with other viewers. Television does not *have* to be a tool for passivity. But human nature is such that when everything is done for us, we don't voluntarily counterbalance with our own activity.

There is a subtle irony at work here. The perfection of reproducing techniques has allowed music to get closer and closer to the listener. The walkman is a good example. Yet, strange as it may seem, while the music becomes physically closer, to the point where it is piped directly into the ear, the listener is farther from the actual musical substance. How greatly can that distance be increased and still allow us to call it the art, the skill of music?

Homogenized Music?
A third, and most important, consideration related to the omnipresence of music is what we could call the problem of pluralism. It is a great privilege to be able to encounter and explore peoples and cultures other than our own. Rapid travel and communication have made it possible to learn about customs and traditions far removed from those we are familiar with. Anthropology and ethnography have enabled us to find out about social structures and traditions in many places the world over. The corollary in cultural spheres, including the arts, has opened up horizons unimagined in previous generations. Ethnomusicology is a relatively new field, and it is still occupied with defining its own premisses, but it has also exposed western musicians to musical practices and traditions from a great diversity of contexts.

Academic disciplines are not the only means to this contact with the outside. Our large cities are show-pieces of cultural diversity, owing to the presence of people from so many different backgrounds, all living relatively close together. Churches and concert halls display some of this diversity as well. Worshippers can actually learn religious songs from many different traditions, simply by asking different ethnic groups to share their music in church. A strong case can be made for the argument that just as learning a foreign language not only helps expose us to another culture but actually expands our way of thinking, so learning another musical

15

culture gives us new insights and enriches our knowledge of the creative process.[6]

Pluralism in music is often a very healthy phenomenon. However, the problems cannot be ignored. There is a kind of Heisenberg principle at work, because when we get too close to the material it tends to modify what we are examining. The availability of music of every kind from all over the world also affects the music itself. Early in 1985 a remarkable series of concerts was held at Carnegie Hall and Avery Fisher Hall in New York City. Twenty-five symphony orchestras and half as many chamber ensembles gathered from all over the world to perform, one after the other. It was a rare opportunity to compare the sounds of the great orchestras from Cleveland, Paris, Toronto, Rome, and elsewhere. How would such different musicians handle the same pieces? It was a unique chance to find out. The answer, however, was a surprising one. They all sounded pretty much the same!

Gone, then, is the distinctiveness of the great orchestras of the past. There is no longer a 'Stokowski sound', or an 'Ansermet sound'. Sir Thomas Beecham used to conduct nineteenth-century French music in a special way. Pierre Monteux had his own colour. But now the sound is not so distinctive. Perhaps this is explained by the increasing travel, the extended tours, the great number of guest conductors whom orchestras experience. Yet we wonder whether at the very moment when this sort of mobility is finally possible, because of our modern means, the point of such exchanges is being lost.

Once again, the key factor here is recorded sound. Before records and tapes it was possible for a musician to do his training without ever being exposed to traditions outside of those of his own country. A conductor coming up through the ranks of the French opera world, for example, would know only the French singers, orchestras and theatres. Today, all this has changed, and it is rare to find a musician who is not well acquainted with the world's renowned soloists. The liability of this sort of exposure is the possibility of homogenized sound. The excitement of being able to see a new orchestra on television may keep us from thinking about the effects it may have on our own artistic development.

This phenomenon is found in the popular music field as

16

well. A case in point is popular music broadcasting in America. AM radio (Amplitude Modulated) makes money exclusively from the advertisements featured all through the programmes. In contrast to this, FM (Frequency Modulated) tends to be private, or sponsored by a handful of companies. The atmosphere is very different between the two. The AM style is more direct, more hard-hitting, whereas FM is more 'intellectual', with more of a mellow style. In 1973 Barry Manilow's 'Could It Be Magic?' appeared on a long-playing record, and was aired on FM radio. The piece begins with a long quotation from Chopin's 'Prelude in C Minor'. Then there is an original song, played with increasing intensity in the succeeding stanzas. Finally the Chopin Prelude comes back at the end. The piece was seven minutes long, very appropriate for FM radio. The record sold well.

Two years later the piece was heard on AM radio. It had the same title, and was billed as 'the same music', but in fact the composer altered it considerably to fit the demands of the AM style. It was shortened to three-and-a-half minutes. The piece was so flexible that Manilow could keep the same 'feeling' while considerably modifying the music. Only a few measures of the Chopin were used. The first few stanzas of the song are eliminated, and we only hear the crescendo of the last few. The Chopin is there briefly at the end. Thus the principal ingredients to 'remember' the piece by are kept, but the whole is modified in order to give it the feeling of an AM hit record. There is even a provision at the end for the disc-jockey to come in, which is standard AM practice. The music fades out appropriately.

A new edition of the same original long-playing record came out, with the feature song 'Could It Be Magic?' advertised on the jacket. But strictly speaking, it was not the song that AM listeners were hearing on their radios. Was this false publicity? The song was 'the same' yet different. The musical material is so flexible that this sort of manipulation is possible.[7] For music to be able to lend itself to this sort of modification, it must be accordingly simple, pliable, not to say without backbone. Music as a consumer product tends to suffer the same fate as packaged foods: the taste is bland.

In his book on technology William Barrett brings up a fascinating episode. In the late 1890s the scientist-scholar

William James visited the summer resort colony in Chautauqua, New York. It was an extraordinary place in many ways. It was meant to be a sort of earthly paradise, with all kinds of features, including evangelical preaching. James relates: 'You have magnificent music—a chorus of seven hundred voices, with possibly the most perfect open-air auditorium in the world. You have every sort of athletic exercise . . . You have kindergartens and model secondary schools . . . You have culture, you have kindness, you have cheapness, you have quality . . .' His irony changes to incisive critique when he goes on to say that he cannot abide 'the atrocious harmlessness of all things'. He would so much rather be in the outside world, with its 'heights and depths, the precipices and steep ideals, the gleams of the awful and the infinite'. He hates the place 'just resting on its oars'. What he specifically says about the arts is most significant. Art must communicate man's struggle. It must bring home to us 'sweat and effort, human nature strained to its uttermost and on the rack, yet getting through alive . . .'.[8]

Thus we have a powerful reminder of the way in which a careless use of technology and other means for the acquisition and manipulation of the substance of art can isolate us from truth. The great diversity of our experience, our struggles, our joys, can be so easily watered down when we let these powerful tools get out of hand. Fortunately, the situation is far from hopeless. In fact, contrary to what certain prophets of doom have predicted, the world is not necessarily heading toward a great melting pot of cultural entities. The danger is there, but complete homogenization has not taken place.

In a unique study of the problem of musical imperialism, the process of change in the popular music of small countries has been analysed by Roger Wallis and Krister Malm.[9] It was shown that large western companies have been able to promote hit records, disco, and so on, using aggressive marketing techniques, in places like Chile, Tunisia, Sri Lanka, Jamaica and Norway. The results are most fascinating. On the one hand, as could be expected, the national folk music suffered. While new technology enabled some of these countries to rediscover some of their own musical traditions, once they come to the surface there is a change. Much national folk music has either been replaced or transformed under the spell of rock and roll. International homogenization, once again. On the other hand, however, national groups emerged, singing their own brand of popular music, not quite like western styles. They had their own flavours, Norwegian, Tunisian, and so on. According to Wallis and Malm, then, the likelihood of developing a global musical culture is small. Such a process would 'continually be "disturbed" by the activities of an underground cultural guerrilla'. This is a very important observation. This cultural guerrilla is the irrepressible human need to define itself over against outside invaders.

Music is so close to the heart of humans that although in some sense it is a universal (very difficult to say how or why!), in another sense it belongs to the essential diversity of human cultural life. I recently had the opportunity of visiting a small country in the heart of West Africa. I was teaching at a seminary there, and one of my courses was on Sub-Saharan ethnomusicology. I used a good many taped examples from different regions. The older members of the audience were delighted, because they recognized many things from their own tribal backgrounds. But the younger ones, having been brought up in the cities, knew only the western superhits, or the African rock bands. As the course went on, I saw more and more interest among the younger ones, and I witnessed a strong desire to rediscover their roots. They saw that it was 'their' music, and it spoke to them in a way other music did not.

How then can we live in a pluralistic world, with all the benefits involved, without blending everything together. How can healthy musical diversity be preserved?

On the Spiritual in Music

One more issue needs to be touched upon before we look into some of the biblical material. For many people there is something about music that calls forth the deepest things of the human spirit. It seems to have special affinities with the sacred. In every culture music holds an important place in worship, prayer and spiritual life. Why is this? Is there something 'divine' about the art of music?

The omnipresence of music in our world forces us to deal with this question as well. On the surface it might appear that music has been completely secularized, along with the rest of our culture. This process can be observed in a number of different ways. Over the last two centuries a serious decline in religious music can be traced in the West. By and large, the great composers have not provided worship music that is really accessible to congregations. In fact, the Church has lost its importance as the mother of the most creative spirits in the arts. Paul Henry Lang goes so far as to say that religious energies are dissipated in the very endeavour of trying to regain religion. The Church has become 'the refuge for all the music unfit for theatre or concert hall'.[10] The judgement is a bit severe, but true in part.

The secularization process can be observed on a smaller scale in the process of change undergone in black American music of the 1960s. The rise of 'soul' music was in direct proportion to the decline of gospel music. Almost all of the great soul singers, from Ray Charles to Aretha Franklin, came out of the Church. The basic structure of the music is the same, but there is a great pull in soul music toward entertainment and worldliness.

A deeper look, however, tells us something a bit different. While it is true that the Christian element in music is on the wane, and that the Church does not have the influence it used to, a religious dimension to much modern music is very noticeable. The invasion itself could be considered a religious factor. Certainly there is an aspect of video-clips which is cultic. They are irrational, often mysterious, with musical high-priests leading in worship. Their electronic ceremonial gear lulls us and cajoles the adepts toward the altar of pleasure. We are using the term religion here in a loose sense. Yet the ingredients are there: a look into the mythic dimension, a rallying-point for the faithful, a tacit message of salvation through music. The recent rock film *Purple Rain* clearly puts forth rock and roll as salvation, portraying it as the answer to the conflicts of the screenplay.

Many of the modern composers are religious in this broader sense as well. Anton von Webern (1883 – 1945), a colleague of Arnold Schönberg, shared the serialists' vision of a music that could bring the listener into a higher sphere, into the 'other'. He was a pantheist, pressing for the 'identity of everything'. The music he advocated was atonal. He developed

20

a musical system which would prevent any centre, any note, any part of the composition from becoming overemphasized. Adherence to his system, respecting the 'round of twelve notes', is 'strict, often burdensome, but it's *salvation!*'[11] He may have been speaking specifically about music's own salvation, in the same way that Schönberg is known to have felt a personal calling to 'save' Western music from its plight. But in Webern's case it is hard to separate this from his belief in a higher spiritual sphere. Webern believed that if music could be strictly egalitarian, the listener would experience what he called 'the Word', a sort of ground of being beyond the visible world. This vision is very close to that of Stockhausen, whom we discussed above.

We are in the strange situation where de-Christianization does not mean the absence of religion, but the presence of new forms of the sacred. Today's Christians must reckon with this presence, and must post their own answers to the pressures of this aspect of modernity. Is there sacred music? If there is, how does it differ from other kinds of music? The question is not a new one, but it comes upon us with a particular force today, especially since there has been a lack of reflection about the arts on the part of Christians for a number of years. Also, secular music, like rock, seems so very far removed from Christian purposes, that the old principles of adapting worldly songs for churchly purposes seem artificial and false. If the 'jazz mass' of the sixties was a strange marriage, Christian rock appears even stranger. In the baroque period the Church could incorporate secular music without controversy, since the styles were so close. The stylistic world of Bach's secular cantata *Was mir behagt*, even though it was written for a hunting party in Saxe Weissenfels, is so close to that of his sacred cantata *Also hat Gott*, composed nineteen years later, that he was able to transfer an aria from the former to the latter with very few changes. In modern times, however, a hundred questions have to be answered before such transfers can even be considered.

2: Jubal's Bequest

No-one denies that much of the world's music is religious in its purpose. Many would even see a 'religious' meaning in all music, at least in a very broad sense. But I want to go further and suggest that the biblical world-view unlocks a number of mysteries about the actual fabric of music, giving us a foundation for a number of crucial aesthetic matters. It is to these considerations that we must now turn.

The Bible is a surprising book. Its authority is not a simple matter to explain. On the whole it does not put forth a well-ordered system of doctrines. It is not an encyclopedia of beliefs, at least in form. It would be a mistake, however, to see it as a random collection of moral teachings or even of historical descriptions of key events in the life of God's people. There is an order to be discovered, even if it is not the order of a modern encyclopedia. Amidst the bewildering diversity of the biblical texts, the poetry, narrative, proverbs, missives, apocalyptic utterances, prayers, and so on, there is a fundamental unity. Throughout the history of biblical interpretation there has been a tendency either to obscure the unity in favour of the diversity, or the diversity in favour of the unity. In the earlier part of our century theologians tended to emphasize the unity of revelation, the uniqueness of the Word of God. A current known as the Biblical Theology Movement traced the grand themes of the Old and New Testaments across each epoch in the history of redemption. Word-books were created which looked at key terms as the various authors employed them, words like Apostle, Church, Messiah. The idea was to uncover the basic meaning of the word through a sweeping overview.

While this was a legitimate undertaking, it tended to neglect the particularities of different authors, genres and periods. More recently the pendulum has swung over to a view which seeks to examine each biblical text, not first of all in relation to others, but as it stands. Words were discovered to have different meanings for different contexts. Syntax and grammatical structure had to be understood before the sense could be brought out. Of course, what is needed is a healthy balance of both approaches. Unity and diversity are not opposed, but complementary. The unity and diversity of the biblical material is not just incidental, but reflects the ultimate nature of the primary author, who is 'one God, in three Persons'. So the authority of the Bible will necessarily be clothed in a form which carries both the unity of its central message, and the diversity of the many facets of truth.

This being the case, looking for clues in the Bible that will lead us to a deeper understanding of music is an investigation which must respect the form of scriptural revelation. It will not do to seek either an abstract uniformity in each verse which says something about music, or an atomistic or random sprinkling of notions. The Bible is a surprising book because its teaching on a particular subject like music is woven into the fabric of its modes and genres. We will discover also that many of the teachings are themselves surprising, and therefore challenging.

Jubal's Apologetic
It would seem natural to assume that music is a gift of God. The reason why so many generations of thinkers have felt all along that there is a special connection between music and the sacred would be explained by the divine nature of the gift. Psalm 87, sung by the Sons of Korah, the specially appointed musicians of the Temple liturgy, is a poetic description of the holy city of Jerusalem, the dwelling-place of God. It is the Psalm from which we derive our hymn, 'Glorious things of thee are spoken, Zion, city of our God.' At the end, the refrain is, 'Singers and dancers alike say, "All my springs are in you."' This confirms our impression! Music and dance are inspired in Zion because God permeates that heavenly place with his outpoured grace.

It is strange to discover quite another teaching from a chapter in the Book of Genesis, which describes the origins of musical activity in the human race. Genesis 4 is best known for its narrative of the murder of Abel by his brother Cain. But the last part of the chapter deals with Cain's family. In a very succinct way, we are told about the descendants of Cain. They were the first-named originators of what we call cultural activity. Enoch's name was given to the first city, which Cain built; Jabal began tent-dwelling and cattle-raising; and Tubal-cain was the first metallurgist. Verse 21 tells us that Jabal's brother Jubal was 'the father of all those who play the lyre and pipe'. The brevity of all these assertions can be frustrating for the modern reader, who wants to know more about the origins of human culture than the biblical author cares to tell him. Many questions are raised. What was a lyre, or a pipe? What branch of the human race are we dealing with, Cro-Magnon, Neanderthal, Mesopotamian? Just the same, some important principles do come out of the text.

First of all, in startling contrast not only to our commonly-held sentiment, but also to religious traditions that surrounded the Jewish People at the time of the writing of this passage, no divine origins for music are affirmed. Jubal was the father of instrumental music, not God. As if to drive the nail further in, we find that Jubal was a descendant of Cain, and not of the godly successor to his slain brother, who was called Seth (v. 25). It is clear, in fact, that a deliberate opposition is intended between the two lines, that of Cain and that of Seth. Cain's descendants invent culture, while Seth's invent worship. At the time of Seth's son, Enosh, the text tells us, 'men began to call upon the name of the Lord' (v. 26). This opposition is not simply an isolated example. As we read further into Genesis we find that often when men are building, creating or doing culture, it is for humanistic purposes. Lamech uses song to boast to his wives about his exploits (4.23–4). The appreciation of feminine beauty led to the corruption of the men of Noah's time (Gen. 6.2–5). The people of the land of Shinar built the Tower of Babel in order to magnify their name above God's (Gen. 11.1–6). Many times these endeavours resulted in the judgement of God, following which a new society of more faithful servants of the Lord is founded.

The first thing we learn from the much neglected fourth chapter of Genesis, then, is that music-making is human activity. The ancient world believed otherwise. The Greeks, who gave us the word itself, have a myth about the origins of music which attributes it to the gods. Apollo's young brother Hermes had stolen some oxen from him, and he used the guts of the animals to make strings. Tying them to the two ends of a turtle shell, he gave us a primeval lyre. He appeased his brother's anger by letting him use it, and he played it with great skill. Thus the gods are directly involved in giving us instruments. It was the same for the *aulos*, a kind of pipe which is found in Asia Minor. This instrument was championed by the Phrygian Olympos, and sometimes the two instruments were used as rivals. Great contests between the gods were established, and judgements were meted out for the lesser musicians.

In the Oriental tradition of the Tao, music itself is believed to have divine qualities. According to Kwang-Hze, the instruments of men are attuned to heavenly forces such as righteousness, propriety and purity. Heaven was the place of the 'Perfect Music', which in turn dispensed the five virtues, the succession of the seasons, and the 'Yin and Yang' which underlay the world's goings on.

The earliest writing about music so far uncovered is in connection with a Hurrian cult love song. It is dated at least at 1800 BC. This text, from the Assyro-Babylonian culture, is interesting from many points of view, but scholars have deciphered a set of musical instructions which describe the strings of an ancient lyre by number. There were seven strings, and each one carried a number except for the fourth, or middle string. This one is given a name. It was designated as '[the god] Ea created it'. Ea was the name of the god of civilization and the arts. There was a direct inspiration from a god in the music because of this arrangement.[1]

The Genesis text gives us a very different approach. The emphasis in the early chapters of Genesis is on the objective nature of the world created by God. He, being essentially different from his creatures, does not relate to the world by mingling with it. Because the world is created, outside of God's nature, as it were, it has a certain self-determination. Not an autonomy, because it remains *God*'s creation, dependent on him. Yet he does not manipulate his creatures, nor do they ever become part of the divine essence.[2] This concept is radically different from those myths which speak of a commingling of divine nature with earthly.

The stories of music's origins we have alluded to are thus very different in their outlook from the Genesis account of Jubal. In the parallel stories of Sumero-Accadian origins, the god *Enki* holds the title of patron of the arts, of singers and musicians. In the biblical account Jubal is both the father of

25

instrumental music and its inventor. His name may mean 'horn', or even 'sound'. This contrast is quite deliberate, and underlines the first part of the double apologetic. Music is man-made, not from divine essence.

A superficial reading of Genesis 4 will overlook the important links that are made with the preceding chapters, texts which deal with the Creation and the Fall. Chapter 4 begins with Adam and Eve's union, wherein the man 'knew' his wife. There is a clear allusion here to the creation mandate of marriage in the second chapter. The man leaves his father and mother and cleaves to his wife, in unashamed knowledge of each other, because God instituted this basic relationship (Gen. 2.23−5). There is continuity in human activity despite the Fall. Agriculture and sheep-raising, the principal work of Cain and Abel, are very close to the activities of Adam and Eve in the Garden. And the language of the fourth chapter itself reminds us of the first order of things. After Cain has killed his brother, the *ground* gives forth cries of blood (v. 10), and this ground will be a curse for Cain, so that his work will be a great burden (vv. 11−12). Nevertheless his work does continue, he must reckon with the ground in his labour, because his vocation is not annulled. He becomes a wanderer on the *earth*, east of Eden, but yet he is protected by God from would-be avengers of his brother (vv. 12−16). The parallels of ground (*adam*) and earth (*eretz*) to the earlier chapters are intended, and help the reader to understand both the difference in the quality of man's relation to the world, because of the Fall, and the continuity with the first mandate of Gen. 1.28, at the dawn of Creation. God had given unfallen man the great commandment to 'be fruitful and multiply, and fill the earth and subdue it . . .' (1.28), and despite the modification which the revolt against God necessarily provoked, there is great continuity with the calling of the first generations of men.

When we arrive at the seventeenth verse of chapter 4, we find the same expression used to describe the union and procreation by Cain and his wife, as we found for Adam and Eve in the first verse. Cain built and named a city for their son Enoch, we are told. Of course, it is difficult to avoid the impression that the city serves partly as a refuge, a place of protection from the threat of exile to which that race had been

26

subjected. In that sense there is an element of alienation from God expressed in this first cultural endeavour. Nevertheless to build a city is a legitimate undertaking, one which would receive the greatest approval possible in the New Jerusalem established by God himself (Heb. 12.13; Rev. 21.2). Human cultural activity is legitimate, even after the Fall. It is not merely a sinful refuge or technological escapism.

It may appear that this teaching on human activity is contradicted by other emphases in Scripture. For example, if music is human activity, what about those marvellous texts which tell of the rest of the creation singing? The Psalms, for example, often speak of music coming from nature:

> . . . let the field exult, and everything in it!
> Then shall all the trees of the wood sing for joy
> before the Lord. (Ps. 96.12)

or:

> Let the floods clap their hands;
> let the hills sing for joy together
> before the Lord. (Ps. 98.8 — 9)

A number of the prophets speak of music in nature as well. The book of Isaiah is particularly full of descriptions of it:

> Sing, O Heavens, for the Lord has done it;
> shout, O depths of the earth;
> break forth into singing, O mountains,
> O forest, and every tree in it! (Isa. 44.23)

We must recognize that this sort of personification is extremely widespread in Scripture. It would be too simple to call it mere metaphor, saying that the Israelite poets were particularly fond of comparing nature to anthropomorphic attributes. The modern reader is tempted either to minimize the significance of the comparison by calling it *mere* metaphor, or, the opposite, to fail to see any difference between this biblical mentality and pantheism. Indeed, many modern interpreters, seeking to defend a sort of dynamic biblical mind-set, maintain that these writers really believed in a singing tree, or a hand-clapping flood. But both of these views miss the point.

The so-called 'nature psalms' are not deifications of nature, but reminders that in every aspect, in every function, the processes of the world are ordered by God and dependent upon him. The *creatureliness* of the universe is taught throughout the Old Testament, and ambiguities on this doctrine are the source of the greatest apostasies. 'The earth is the Lord's and the fullness thereof' is the fundamental frame of reference within which all of Israel's perception of nature operates (Ps. 24.1).

Yet God's presence, as he reveals himself in nature, is clearly perceived by believing Israel.[3] This is the crucial point. God's glory is *revealed*, and his salvation *taught*, through nature. There is a cosmic dimension to God's glory and to his redemption. Because of this, the psalmist really does *hear* the Lord's voice thundering upon the waters (Ps. 29.3—7). He really *sees* God covered with light as with a garment and riding a chariot of clouds (Ps. 104.2—3). This is not mere metaphor, but poetic truth. Not for one instant did the psalmist fall into a kind of nature religion. Often, the very psalms which push the personification of nature to extremes are also the ones with the clearest declarations of God's distinct sovereignty over the world (Ps. 29.10—11; 104.1, 9, 24, 27—30). God feeds the flocks, gives wine to men, judges the world, and orders all events by the word of his mouth (Ps. 147).

The final purpose of the poet's experience is praise and adoration of the God of Creation and the God of Salvation. These are the psalmodies of redeemed Israel, the Lord's people, called to recognize him as author of salvation as well as creator of the world. What they see in nature is the work of his hand, his wisdom, his greatness. Nature is a witness to these qualities because God reveals them in it, not because of some inherent principle or mechanism which 'emits' divine power. Only in communion with him, the source of revelation, is it possible to see and hear these things. Nor are they a *projection* of the believer. They are an actual finding.

Human Activity
There is a subtle, but important difference here between the biblical emphasis and the once popular idea of the 'music of the spheres'. We have seen examples of this view in some of the ancient myths. Pythagoras gave the idea its classical

28

expression. According to him the motion of the planets depended in a mysterious way on music. Not music that could be heard by human ears, but sounds which were linked to mathematical principles and which were the distant generators of human music. At least one biblical passage seems to corroborate this view at first reading:

> Where were you when I laid the foundation of the earth?
>   Tell me, if you have understanding.
> Who determined its measurements — surely you know!
>   Or who stretched the line upon it . . .
> when the morning stars sang together,
>   and all the sons of God shouted for joy? (Job 38.4 — 5, 7)

However, according to biblical parallels (see Isa. 14.12; Dan 8.10; Rev. 12.4), and according to the usage in the Book of Job itself, the 'morning stars' are angelic hosts. The angels sang at the creation of the world! We do not know much about heavenly beings from Scripture. But we do know that they are creatures like men, not demi-gods, with powers and abilities which men cannot perhaps well imagine, but with personalities as well. There are other occasions at which angels sang the praise of God. The best-known is recorded in the Gospel of Luke, at the birth of the Christ-child (Luke 2.13 — 14; see Zech. 4.7; Rev. 4.8 — 11, 19.1 — 8).

The problem, then, with finding a 'rival' source of music in nature is not that there is no music there, at least in some sense, but that we forget music's creatureliness, and man's crucial role as primary agent in the development of the musical process. Nature does not generate music independently from man, or from human agency (or angelic agency). This is the mistake, I believe, in Jean-Philippe Rameau's Enlightenment approach to musical aesthetics. Rameau (1683 — 1764) has been neglected by audiences and even by historians. There is great beauty in his music, despite his own drive toward rationalistic consistency. Indeed he was dominated by the ideals of the eighteenth century, and sought to explain music, along with the other arts, in terms of Cartesian principles:

> In order fully to enjoy the effects of music, one must completely leave off from oneself, and to evaluate it one must relate to the principle by which one is affected. That principle is nature itself;

29

it is from her that we acquire the sentiment that moves us in all our musical activities; she has made us a gift of it which we might call *instinct*.[4]

His best known theoretical work is the *Treatise on Harmony Reduced to its Natural Principles*, written in 1722 (the same year as Johann Sebastian Bach published the first volume of his *Well-tempered Clavier*. What a contrast in world-views!). This book is foundational for the European views on harmony that followed, for two hundred years. In it he proposed reducing all harmony to a fundamental tone, and then to its natural subdivisions. This principle can be understood by stretching a string, and dividing it in half, in thirds, etc., then plucking it to find the corresponding pitch intervals generated. He found that the simplest ratios corresponded with the basic intervals of our diatonic scale . . . or almost. He also established the classical theory of functional harmony. Building chords with the triad, three notes (do-mi-so, for example), the same natural principles led him to isolate the principle functions of the principle chords, known as tonic, dominant, and sub-dominant.

While sharply criticized by his musical rival, the philosopher Jean-Jacques Rousseau (1712—1778), it turns out that the quarrel was between two ideological cousins. While on the surface Rousseau disagreed with Rameau's taste for French opera, instead of the fashionable Italian opera, underneath he shared Rameau's immanentism.[5] His own operas (Rousseau was a skilled composer, if not a great one) stressed nature, and not the traditional mythological subjects. He also theorized about his 'plausible hypothesis' of the innocence of natural man.

In fact deriving musical norms from empirical observations in nature never quite matched the reality of musical practice. The ear had another agenda! While Rameau's principle of the stretched string worked for the octave and the fifth, it broke down for thirds and other intervals. As every piano-tuner knows, even at the level of tightening or loosening the strings of the harpsichord or piano, certain compensations, compromises and inconsistencies with 'nature' must be used if the instrument is really to be harmonious.

The problem with deriving music from 'natural' principles

is not that human beings must never work with the natural world. Absurdities would follow such radicalism. No technology would be possible in music at all. The problem is rather with a certain view of nature. The philosophical uses of the term 'nature' are varied and complex, but what I particularly want to warn against is natural*ism*, that is, the general drive to search for ultimate meaning in an autonomous nature. Accordingly, music's meaning would be limited to an immanentistic approach, without any possible reference to an external truth, one revealed by an outside point of origin.

Rameau's immanentism led him to seek the essence of musical order in nature as he understood it. Romanticism reacted against his kind of rationalism, but it did not fundamentally escape his immanentism. The Romantics longed for the infinite, to be sure, but it was more of a youthful intoxication with a better world, a world which could be discovered through communion with nature. Nature, in their view, functioned as a sort of revelation of human experience, an extended ego. Thus neither in the natural law concept of Rameau, nor in the Romantic longing do we find a breach with naturalism.

Intelligent human response, so important to the meaning of music, does not exclude the manipulation of nature. But it puts the focus 'above' rather than 'below'. My problem with the excessive use of electronics in modern music stems from this. It represents an unhealthy focus on the power and effects of mechanical music production, and not a human response to the Creator. The modern fascination with this power carries with it the risk of becoming dependent on it, the risk of a kind of idolatry.

This problem is not a new one. The motets of the Parisian school in the twelfth and thirteenth centuries, while in many ways displaying bold and daring features, seemed to have been severely limited by the abstract and unlyrical quality of their compositional basis. Based on a scholastic concept of music, whose history cannot be gone into here,[6] the idea consists in building three musical levels which are almost not at all related, in the same metrical time. Two melodies are imposed over a third one, whose theme is the *cantus firmus* from Gregorian chant. The *cantus* had to follow a particular academic prescription. The metre had to be either iambic, spondaic, trochaic, dactylic, or anapaestic, with rests between the sections so that mathematically there was a regular sequence. There was no regard for the *musical* rhythm, or the melodic patterns suggested: 'Here one sees scholastic law and orderly system enforced. It is immaterial whether the system suits the melody or not; the *cantus firmus* has to conform and is forcibly cut up accordingly.'[7] Of course, there is a kind of fantastic side to this, which appeals to the Gothic spirit of the times, forcibly welding together three totally different melodies, sung in three different languages, generally. But it is no wonder that a reaction set in, in favour of a more lyrical, popular music. The troubadours of France and the minnesingers of Germany were not exactly in competition with the scholastic music of the Church, but let us say that the Church and the convent schools did not encourage this lyric poetry and music.

By these remarks I do not want to give the impression that we ought to reject all styles of music which have a mathematical basis. We are simply moving along in the argument, trying to emphasize the contrast between the biblical norm of man-made music and the problems encountered when this is forgotten. This explains, I think, some of our uneasiness with the kinds of reproducing devices we looked at in the previous chapter. The great push for synthesized sounds and electronically determined tonal effects today must be measured against the biblical emphasis on the human agency. Without yielding to the temptation of black and white judgements, let us simply raise the question here, and leave it for further consideration.

Looking again at the Bible, one more objection to the thesis of human origins might be raised. If Scripture does not teach a natural source, then what about the fact of God's own inspiration of music? Not only would general theological considerations seem to oblige us to recognize God's primary authorship of art and culture, but there are indications in Scripture that God himself practises the art of music. At least one text makes specific reference to it:

Jehovah thy God is in the midst of thee, a mighty one who will save; he will rejoice over thee with joy; he will rest in his love; he will joy over thee with singing (Zeph. 3.17. ASV).

32

This is a most wonderful passage. God rejoices over his people by singing! No-one would deny the attribution of 'emotions' to God. As a personal being, he is often spoken of in terms of feelings, anger, love, and so on. Music is a manifestation of emotions, and there is no reason to shy away from attributing song to the Lord. But two things need to be said which raise difficulties for the idea of the directly divine origins of music.

First, the context here is not one in which God's creative acts are being considered. This section of the prophecy of Zephaniah deals with the restoration of unfaithful Israel, and the ultimate return to God's presence they will experience. There is no teaching about origins here. All that could be suggested is that if human beings make music by singing, *it is no coincidence* that song can also be attributed to their maker. The second consideration goes deeper. Our verse begins by saying that God is in the midst of his people. This is not an isolated expression. It is found throughout the Old Testament, and is an announcement of the very Incarnation, Immanuel, God-with-us (Isa. 7.14). Psalm 22.22 goes further, and declares that this incarnate redeemer will praise God in the midst of the assembly. The New Testament Book of Hebrews attributes this same function to Jesus Christ (Heb. 2.12; see Rom. 15.8 — 10). Christ is pictured as leading his brethren in songs of worship. There is a rich theology of salvation here, and we shall explore some of it later. But here let us simply notice that the Zephaniah passage has its key in the teaching on the incarnation. God, in Jesus Christ, who stands in the midst of the congregation of the redeemed, rejoices over his people with singing. A case for direct divine origins cannot be made, then, by appealing to this biblical-theological theme. Christ leads in song, but that is not the same as saying that God originally inspired music.

The Divine Calling
Jubal's bequest does not end here! It is a double apologetic. If on the one hand it is asserted that music's father is a man, God's ultimate authorship of the arts is asserted as well. Genesis 4 speaks against divinizing art, but it also speaks against secularizing it. Although the Fall has troubled man's pursuit of the original mandate of Genesis 1.28, it has not

33

interrupted it, contrary to our first impressions. We have seen some of the ways in which the fourth chapter stands in continuity with the first three, and especially with 1 and 2, the creation chapters. We saw that human tasks continued right on into the history of early humanity. But in the same way, this continuity applies to the central emphasis of the first chapters, which is that *God* ordains human activity. When Adam 'knew' his wife, she bore a son 'with the help of the Lord' (4.1). From this remark we learn that Eve saw in this birth the beginning of a promise fulfilled, the promise of salvation which she had first heard as a curse on the serpent (3.15). But she also realized that the mandate to be fruitful and multiply was still in order (1.28). Replenishing the earth would be possible after all. Also the work engaged in by the sons of the first couple was no doubt a continuation of Adam's occupation. Keeping sheep was pointed out by God either directly or indirectly (3.21), and agriculture was also divinely ordered (2.9, 15). It is often wrongly assumed that the difference between Cain's disposition and Abel's was a matter of the vocation each practised: that keeping sheep permitted the sacrifice of animals, with the faith in expiation entailed, whereas working the soil was less spiritual. It is true that the Lord respected Abel and his offering, but not Cain and his. But the reason is not in *what* they offered, but *how* they offered it.[8] The Book of Hebrews confirms this, by describing Abel as a man of faith, but not Cain (11.4). It is not even certain that sacrifice for atonement is in view at all. More likely, these offerings by the first sons of Adam were especially thank-offerings. This being so, another link is established with the first chapters of Genesis, because man was to work in order to worship God from the beginning. The Sabbath was hallowed for man's rest-in-worship (Gen. 2.3 with Exod. 20.8 – 11; Acts 20.7). Creation was a gift of God (Gen. 1.29), but always as a 'blessing', that is, in God's presence, and for his glory (1.28, see 2.15 – 17).

Cain himself, despite his alienation from God, recognized the perspective of worship in human occupations. He named his son 'Enoch', meaning 'consecration' (4.17). The early development of culture, then, stood in continuity with the order of Creation before the Fall. What do we make of the contrast that is established between the various activities of

Cain's sons, including music-making, and the principal virtue of Seth, Adam's believing son? This line originated public worship: 'At that time men began to call upon the name of the Lord' (4.26).

Certainly the comparison is deliberate. But it would be false to derive from this opposition an absolute antagonism between 'worship' and 'culture', as some have done. First of all, the immediate comparison is not with all culture, but with perverted culture. Lamech boasts to his wives, using poetry, perhaps set to music (4.23—4). It is his attitude rather than his art which is in contrast to Seth's children. And second, worship in the Old Testament is united indissolubly with various cultural dimensions, especially poetry and music, but also architecture and dance. Third, the idea of worship as spiritual and culture as carnal derives far more from a platonic dualism than from biblical anthropology. Some commentators have noticed the relative silence of the New Testament on matters related to the arts, and have concluded from that that there is something less spiritual about cultural pursuits. Some have gone so far as to say that the arts were visible signs of the invisible Christ, so that once he has come the reality replaces the images and our worship is spiritual in the narrowest sense.

Yet the New Testament is not so silent as it might appear on matters pertaining to the arts. Jesus, after all, was a carpenter. The disciples sang hymns with him after meals (Matt. 26.30). Our Lord's teaching was full of metaphors referring to the arts. He even compared his audience to children who refused to dance to a tune! (Matt. 11.16—17). And furthermore, the most important consideration regarding the *relative* absence of New Testament teaching on the arts is that the Old Testament was not abrogated in the New, only fulfilled (Matt. 5.17). It is well known that the famous series of contrasts in the Sermon on the Mount between what 'you have heard' and what 'I say to you' is not a contrast between the Old and New Testament ethics, but between legalistic Pharisaical interpretations of the Old Testament and Jesus's (correct) understanding of it. A high regard for the Law of God is characteristic of the teaching of all the New Testament authors. Even the Apostle Paul, known for his sharp attacks against the Judaizer sects, does not call in question the

35

primary function of the Law (see Rom. 3.31; 7.7; 13.10; Gal. 5.22−3).

Jubal's music-making is good in itself. His legacy is not only legitimate but mandatory. The disincarnate spirituality which relegates cultural pursuits to luxury is out of place in the Old Testament outlook. An interesting consideration might be raised. The Genesis 4 passage mentions *instrumental* music, but nothing is said about *vocal* music. This seems the more strange in that so much that relates to music in the Bible has to do with song. There are only a few references to instrumental music in its pure form. The main reason for this lies in the expression 'father' which is attributed to Jubal. In the biblical view, everyone can sing, but not everyone belongs to the family of musicians. Everyone is called to participate in the enjoyment of music, but not everyone is qualified to be called a musician. This is not a kind of élitist privilege, but a genuine vocation, to be accomplished with skill and hard work. The very idea of a family of musicians precludes élitism. So calling attention to the instruments focuses on the specific art of music to be developed by those who belong to that family, in the same way that having cattle (4.20) focuses on those who belong to the family of herdsmen. All are not qualified in the same way. Adam could probably sing (2.23 is likely to be a song), but is not the father of every skill.

Music, then, is a divine calling. Not in some mystical, individualistic way, but because of the structure of the cultural mandate. The 'decision' to make man in the image of God, according to Genesis 1.26−7, is closely connected with God's purposes for the human race. We shall want to look carefully at the nature of the commission addressed to humankind, in order to understand more about the place of music in human life. But first let us notice the heavenly orientation of this great moment at the dawn of human existence. In continuity with the previous stages of the creation week, it is God who 'says', and it happens (1.26). But in contrast to the former occasions, the plural is used, 'Let us make man in our image, after our likeness'. While it is not possible to be categorical, it would seem that God was addressing the heavenly assembly of angelic hosts. This view fits the context better than the traditional trinitarian interpretation of the plural.[9] This is a momentous occurrence. The judicial council of heavenly beings is brought in on it, because man is about to be created in God's own image. And the purposes of mankind are immediately established. He is to have dominion over the created world and subdue it (1.26, 28).

The calling of humankind is determined not only by the command of God ('let them have dominion'), but by the blessing of God (1.28). In the Old Testament, blessing meant the special presence of God's Spirit on a person or a group. God would put his name on his people in order to lavish his peace and his grace upon them. This is beautifully summed up in the great Mosaic blessing of Numbers 6.22−7, where the three-fold name of God is invoked, and rests on the people. It is God's very face shining on them in his favour. These lines in Genesis are rich in divine perspective. God makes man, and God blesses him. He also orders him to subdue the earth, but this is made possible because God himself gives man every plant, every tree, the context in which he is to work. The account of the creation of the first couple in Genesis 2 (not a 'second creation account' as it is sometimes supposed,[10]) underscores the same perspective. God made man, gave him the breath of life, placed him in a beautiful garden, and gave him the mandate to till it and keep it (2.7−15). God makes the animals, and brings them to Adam to see what he would call them (2.19). He provides man's companion in a sovereign, loving way, so that even marriage and social life are not just human discoveries.

Music, insofar as it belongs to human, cultural activity, is a divine calling. Even fallen Adam could not escape his obligations as a culture-builder. Despite the pain of labour after the fall (3.17−19), despite the rebellious orientation of much cultural activity (4.22−4), by God's grace, we are still called to build culture, to enjoy it, to exercise the functions outlined in the original mandate. Jubal's double apologetic is clear: music is human activity, but it is also a divine calling.

Mere Culture
Up until this point we have been describing music as cultural activity, without attempting to justify the connection. Just what is culture, and how is music to be considered a cultural activity? In fact this is a most difficult question. Many people who hear the term 'culture' think of 'the arts'. 'Cultural

enrichment' means going to a museum, a play, or a concert. If culture is activity which is beyond biological functions, then the arts have a special place, no doubt. But it is not right to overlook other, equally human activities, any more than the Genesis 4 passage does. In addition to the arts, one cannot ignore such parallel traits in mankind as the ability to exploit technologies, customs, and to live within specific social patterns. Such very different things as using Arabic numerals, singing the blues, wearing a red shirt, and going to the local pub are involved. Whereas a few decades ago anthropologists sought to identify cultural traits in far-away, non-western areas, the modern agenda for study includes inner-city gangs, ritual traditions and migrant field labourers.

The problem to be faced is really one of where to draw the line. What, in other words, *is not* cultural? The tendency in modern anthropology is to lump almost everything together as culture. A. L. Kroeber, still a standard reference, defines culture 'negatively', drawing attention to what it is not: 'Put this way around, culture might be defined as all the activities and non-physiological products of human personalities that are not automatically reflex or instinctive.'[11] This obliges him to include speech, knowledge, beliefs, customs, arts, technologies, ideals and rules. While there are no doubt cultural dimensions to all of these, it is dangerous to group all of them into the one ball of wax.

Language, for example, is most certainly replete with signs, symbols, and metaphors which reveal cultural origins. Each social group has its favourite parables, its chosen images to describe experiences of reality. But language, in biblical teaching, is more than a system of symbols and metaphors. 'Without an accepted order of reality to which conceptual language refers, the deviation that constitutes the metaphor could not be recognized.'[12] The use of language is so fundamentally connected with human nature that it is not included in the cultural mandate of Gen. 1.28. It does not seem appropriate to think of language as having a human 'father' in the second generation, in the same way as cultural pursuits do.

The other danger in the culture-as-everything definition is that religion is inevitably thrown into the bag. But the essence of religion cannot be considered a cultural phenomenon, even though culture is involved at many levels. Again, modern anthropology often sees religious commitment as only one 'dimension' of human activity. Like morals, it may serve the very important purpose of ascribing meaning and significance to human life, but religion still belongs to human invention.[13] In the biblical framework, religion cannot be reduced either to culture, to language, or to social or biological needs. It is a response to God's presence, to his person, to his revelation. Religion operates within a covenant structure that is universal, not culturally conditioned. This is not to say that culture does not help shape that response. In fact at the heart of cultural vision and activity there is a core place of religion, which gives meaning and sense to culture.[14] Religion necessarily functions *in* culture, since human beings are cultural creatures. But it is not a pure function of culture.

Even after the fall, religion continues to orient cultural activity. As we have seen, the sons of Cain did not erect neutral cultural traditions. The Tower of Babel was meant to 'make a name for ourselves' in resistance to the God who could unleash the elements in a judgemental flood (Gen. 11.4). The authority and glory of the kingdoms delivered to Satan were offered to Christ in their unredeemed forms in the temptation scene (Luke 4.5 – 7). But certainly the lordship of the devil meant a religious orientation. Religion is not an area or a sphere of life, it is a basic direction. When the Apostle Paul tells the Corinthians, 'whether you eat or drink, or whatever you do, do all to the glory of God' (1 Cor. 10.31) he clarifies the difference. It is possible to eat and drink in two ways. It all depends on one's basic commitments. Not that it ends there. Eating customs, manners, traditions, may be reflections of that basic orientation. Such seemingly neutral habits as eating with the left hand in India, or feasting in the 'presence of my enemies' in ancient Israel, do have religious significance. As missiologist J. H. Bavinck once pointed out, 'culture is religion made visible.'[15]

Image and Dominion
These conclusions are borne out by the biblical materials. It is apparent, and recent Old Testament scholarship tends to confirm this,[16] that there is an important connection between being in the image of God and having dominion over the

creation. But dominion is not a simple concept. It is neither the abusive domination over the world that might lead to the destruction of its ecological systems, nor the slavish fear of going too near to its veiled secrets. The real model is God himself, as he creates and then rules over the world. Psalm 8 expresses astonishment at the thought that finite man could be invested with such authority. The Psalmist has understood the wonder of man's lordship within the ultimate lordship of the Creator:

> Yet thou hast made him little less than God,
>> and dost crown him with glory and honour.
> Thou hast given him dominion over the works of thy hands;
>> thou hast put all things under his feet,
> all sheep and oxen,
>> and also the beasts of the field,
> the birds of the air, and the fish of the sea,
>> whatever passes along the paths of the sea.
> O Lord, our Lord,
>> how majestic is thy name in all the earth!
>
> (Ps. 8.5—9)

Human beings have been given an office, one which requires the exercise of cultural gifts in a religious orientation. This office can only be maintained because God is himself the supreme ruler of his creation. He is not away at a distance, but present, so as to order all things, and, especially, in order to have covenant fellowship with human beings. Meredith Kline has pointed out the important connection between the image of God in humankind and the presence of God in his creation, a presence first expressed in terms of the Spirit of God hovering over the face of the deep (see Gen. 1.2). He points out that the same Hebrew verb is used as in Deuteronomy 32.11, which describes God's leading of Israel to Canaan as an eagle protecting its young. Kline brings a good deal of biblical data together to show that God's presence is one of glory and power. Because God has created, his presence in glory is a revelation of the deepest truth, usually veiled within a 'theophanic cloud' (see, for example, Ezek. 1.1ff; 3.12ff; 10.1ff; etc.). That deep truth is God's glorious rule over all creatures:

40

When the inner reality veiled within the theophanic cloud is revealed, we behold God in his heaven. The world of the Glory theophany is a dimensional realm normally invisible to man, where God reveals his presence as the King of glory enthroned in the midst of myriads of heavenly beings . . . Thus, the Spirit-Glory of Genesis 1.2b answers to the invisible heavens of Genesis 1.1 and represents a coming forth of the Lord of glory out of invisibility into a special earth-oriented and adapted manifestation to create and consummate, to reveal himself in earth history as Alpha and Omega.[17]

Man as the image of God reflects this glorious rule. He has a royal office, exercising dominion over God's world in the name of God and to his glory. In fact, man is a kind of royal priest, who stands before God and brings all the fruits of his dominion to him as an adoration-offering.[18] Culture receives its full meaning within this context.

Of course there is more to the story. There is a social dimension to culture-building, and a geographical one as well. 'Let *them* have dominion,' the ordinance specifies (Gen. 1.26). Furthermore, God created human beings male and female, and told them to 'be fruitful, multiply, and fill the earth.' (1.27 − 8).[19] From the beginning, then, the exercise of dominion was to have a familial and communal dimension. That is another reason for calling Jabal and Jubal fathers. Culture-building is not seen in Scripture as the activity of individuals, nor is the meaning of culture something that can be determined without taking into account the social structure of those who engage in it. While Emile Durkheim and his followers exaggerated the social dimension of culture by *reducing* all culture, including religion, to a symbolification of the social structures of a group, others have fallen into the opposite extreme of divorcing culture from the social bonds of those who build it.

Finally, there is a geographical aspect to the dominion mandate. Human beings were to multiply and replenish *the earth*. Even after the Fall this has been realized. A provision was made from the beginning for the tremendous, bewildering diversity of cultural expression. Each family, each clan, each tribe, cities, nations, whatever contours the social organization of the human race would take on, each entity would know a different cultural expression. No demonstration of this is needed, because we live 'after the fact'. But it is important to see that the divine intention for diversity was there from the beginning. Of course, that diversity was to have been explored within the unity of the human family. But with the Fall, cultural diversity has been exaggerated, and turned into means of erecting barriers between peoples. The same can presumably be said for languages. Nevertheless, even in a fallen world, there remains a certain unity in the essential purpose of culture, which is to seek God. In many cases there is only a dim memory of that purpose, but it is strong enough for the Apostle Paul to use it as a point of contact with non-Jewish cultures in the early days of Christian missions:

> And he made from one every nation of men to live on all the face of the earth, having determined allotted periods and the boundaries of their habitation, that they should seek God, in the hope that they might feel after him and find him. (Acts 17.26−7)

Paul's message, along with that of every New Testament author, was that the true sense of the image of God could be regained, and real dominion rediscovered, in Jesus Christ, 'who will change our lowly body to be like his glorious body, by the power which enables him even to subject all things to himself' (Phil. 3.21). Christ is indeed the ultimate image of God (Heb. 1.3), who opens the door for our own true exercise of dominion, beginning in this world, and culminating in the next. In fact, Christ is considered by the author of the Epistle to the Hebrews to be *the man* of Psalm 8, who, because he has everything in subjection to him, is able to lead us back into true dominion, making our cultural activity, in all its diversity, committed to God from the heart (Heb. 2.5−9). And music is specifically included in the programme! (Heb. 2.10−13).

Music as Culture
As we move into the centre of our discussion, we realize that there are at least two problems which make definitions of music very difficult. The first is the one we have been examining, the nature of culture. We have clarified a number of things. Yet it still may not be clear what exactly constitutes

42

cultural activity and what does not. Is government a cultural phenomenon? What about belonging to the Baptist Church? We have tried to point out that values and religious convictions are not, properly speaking, cultural entities. Yet it is clear that certain values, and even religious practices, can be culture-specific. The relation of values, including basic, religious criteria, to culture cannot easily be defined. Perhaps it is best to use a fairly dynamic, or open-ended model. Rather than the dualistic concept of content and form, whereby the 'value' involved is put into various types of 'cultural clothing', it might be more helpful to speak of a continuum. At one end, the starting point, there are basic commitments. These determine where we stand in relation to God and his covenant demands. Then, along the line, the particular expressions of our beliefs begin to take shape in terms of paradigms, clusters which form the mental grids, the 'lenses' through which we look at things. Finally, toward the other end, we find customs, skills, social conventions and the like. If we keep this picture in mind, culture would belong somewhere from the middle to the 'customs' end. But the idea is that there is a dynamic flow all along. Music is cultural, *in that sense*, if our model is valid.

The second problem is one of 'is-ought'. If we follow the biblical norms for our definition of culture, and thus our view of music, we are faced with the directives, or ideals, on the one hand, and the actual practice of music on the other. One is as it should be (provided we have understood it correctly!) and the other is as it is in a fallen world. What do we make of the electronic sounds generated from the sophisticated machines at the IRCAM Centre in Paris, which claim not only to be music, but to be today's most authentic sounds? Ethnomusicologists complain, often rightly so, that missionaries refuse to respect indigenous musical styles, imposing their own western traditions on the converts. But are all styles equally suitable for the praise of God? How does one adopt the Inuit Esquimo 'throat-game' music to hymnody? What about Thai Buddhist chant? As we seek to identify music that we know with the biblical ideal for this cultural activity, we will inevitably be confronted with *our own* paradigms and cultural grids. Much of the following material will therefore be suggestive rather than definitive. Yet a number of principles ought to emerge which will help us accomplish the goals of this study.

Jubal's bequest is music as culture. Music is not primarily *in* culture. It *is* cultural activity. 'Music is perceived through cultural canalization and is defined by specific groups who participate in particular genres.'[20] What we generally understand to be music, whatever its ethnic origin, fits the biblical view of culture, especially in its focus on dominion by God's image-bearer. The standard dictionary definitions, however, usually reveal western biases which cannot stand up to empirical observation. For example, Webster's *New Collegiate Dictionary* (1977) defines music as 'the science or art of ordering tones or sounds in succession, in combination, and in temporal relationships to produce a composition having unity and continuity'. Science and art do not really apply to tribal cultures in which music may serve a ritual purpose that is far closer to religious ceremony than 'composition'. Also, 'unity and continuity' might describe music from many cultures aptly enough, but then it would also describe non-human sounds as well. Unity and continuity are notions that cover so much, that they do not really describe anything at all. If we are to be literal, a dog-bark is a sort of 'ordering [of] tones or sounds in succession, in combination, and in temporal relationships'. So much is assumed, with the words 'science and art' that the rest seems to go without verification. And yet what is missing in this kind of definition is the cultural dimension.

A more useful approach would be to define music as 'a complex of activities, ideas and objects that are patterned into culturally meaningful sounds recognized to exist on a level different from secular communication'.[21] Here music is recognized as being shaped by the culture of which it is a part. In fact, each culture decides what is and what is not music. It cannot exist for itself or by itself. It is human activity, or rather, human activities. Also, this definition seems to fit the idea of dominion which is so integral to the image of God. The activities are *patterned*, or ordered, into sounds that are meaningful. This is important, because it conceives of music-making as an *art* (man-made skill). However, there is still something missing here. The definition stops at what is 'culturally meaningful' without suggesting

44

that there is more. If the only musical meaning is cultural, then nothing can prevent the pitfall of relativism.

Here we would plead in favour of our continuum, belief-paradigm-culture.[22] However, culture in the biblical sense is not neutral. It has its place within the total framework of the covenant. The term 'covenant' is unique. It refers to a relationship in which God rules, and man responds. Man can, and does, deviate from the covenant, but he cannot escape its reality, so that even his revolt against it is at some level in terms of it. The meaning-structure of music, which is cultural activity, is rooted in the covenant. 'Belief' may operate with sympathy for the covenant, therefore in obedience to the covenant God, or with antipathy for it and him. Unbelief is a kind of faith. The meaning of cultural activity is always along the line of our continuum, beginning with belief. In other words, it can never simply be contained within the bounds of culture itself, as the definition above suggests. Yet it never is expressed a-culturally either. *Music, then, is human, cultural activity, ordered by the covenant, in the aspect of sound.*

Generalizations beyond this point may be dangerous! Is music art? Or is it one of *the arts*? It all depends, of course, on what is meant by 'art'. In a way we are dealing with a very ambiguous concept. Where does art begin and other activities end? Is cooking an art? What about paving a road? Is football an art? In another way, however, we all know more or less what art is when we see it. We can see that a painter, or even a jewellery-maker, is doing something special that the athlete is not doing. Even though we may speak of a 'beautiful serve' in tennis, the sportsman's first object is not aesthetics, whereas the artist's is.

The Bible does not use the term 'art' or 'artist' very often. When it does it may be pejorative, referring to idols and objects 'made by human hands' (Acts 17.24−5). Yet it does recognize an activity, and even a calling, which could be called artistic. When the tabernacle was being built, God himself appointed the craftsmen to fashion the artwork:

The Lord said to Moses, 'See, I have called by name Bezalel the son of Uri, son of Hur, of the tribe of Judah: and I have filled him with the Spirit of God, with ability and intelligence, with knowledge and all craftsmanship, to devise artistic designs, to work in gold, silver, and bronze, in cutting stones for setting, and in carving wood, for work in every craft.' (Exod. 31.1−5)

Although we are dealing with craft, rather than what western culture would call 'high art', it must be pointed out that not everyone is called to perform it, not everyone has the gift of the Spirit of God to carry it out. Notice that not only the skills are singled out, but also the art-objects, gold, silver, bronze, etc. There is no doubt that Hebrew culture in Mosaic times had a strong sense of the uniqueness of artistic calling.

Art in the Bible is a circumscribed activity within the cultural mandate. It has to do with invention, even play, but especially with skill. In the famous episode where Saul was suffering from an evil spirit (1 Sam. 16.14−23), the cure was to seek out a man who could play the lyre skilfully. More will be said about David's 'music therapy' in a later chapter, but here what is of interest is the nature of his reputation. He was a skilled instrumentalist (vv. 16, 18), but was also 'a man of valour, a man of war, prudent in speech, and a man of good presence; and the Lord is with him.' (v.18). We might say, he was not only a good technician, but well endowed with other qualities that would win him favour in Saul's service. The warrior-poet was not unknown in the ancient world, but David was a special case of one divinely called as an artist. His art included the ability to soothe a tormented soul. And as we know, his art made him one of Jubal's worthiest sons. We owe him many of the Psalms, and also the appointment of the permanent musicians' offices for cultic service (1 Chron. 16.4−7). His skill must have been exceptional, since his reputation was widespread. But as a working musician, he played 'day by day' (1 Sam. 18.10). It may even be that David made his own instruments. Certainly he knew a good deal about them. In later times, the 'instruments of David' become a kind of standard, even an ideal. When David was old he prescribed the offices of the Levites to his son Solomon. Among other duties, four thousand of them were appointed to 'offer praises to the Lord with the instruments *which I have made* for praise (1 Chron. 23.5). The Hebrew word can indeed signify *to make*, in the sense of fabricate. But it can also mean *to prescribe* or *appoint*. In any case, the 'instruments of David' referred to the high quality of what David had endorsed (2 Chron. 29.26; see also Amos 6.5, where inventing instruments like David is condemned as pretentious folly).

Although individuals and families (like the Levites) may be called to do music, the post-Renaissance distinction between the craftsman and the genius was unknown in biblical teaching. The biblical notion of calling excludes all such status-orientation. The same is true for the very place of art within the cultural mandate. Art is neither higher nor lower in the order of divinely-ordained activities than any other legitimate cultural endeavour. This is corroborated by the nature of the smaller group of musicians appointed by David to 'prophesy under the direction of the king' (1 Chron. 25.1 – 8). This group was probably selected according to ability, as well as professional training (v. 7). They were divided, in turn, into 'wards' consisting of twelve musicians each, with a group leader at the head of the ward. Not only were they a kind of guild, with all of the commitment to their calling which that implies, but there were different roles within the guild, according to musical greatness, and ability to teach (v. 8).

Sacred or Secular?

It is sometimes assumed that because the music of praise is spoken of with the highest admiration, other functions are somehow less noble. Indeed, there is no greater joy than when God meets with his people, with all the musical atmosphere in accompaniment. When the ark of the Lord was brought back to Jerusalem, David 'danced before the Lord with all his might' (2 Sam. 6.14), and there was shouting, the sounds of horns, trumpets, cymbals, harps and lyres being the exuberant accompaniment (1 Chron. 15.28). It is difficult to imagine the sheer joy of this occasion, when at last God had favoured his people with the visible sign of his presence:

> Then on that day David first appointed that thanksgiving be sung to the Lord by Asaph and his brethren.
> O give thanks to the Lord, call on his name,
>   make known his deeds among the peoples!

47

Sing to him, sing praises to him,
    tell of all his wonderful works!
Glory in his holy name;
    let the hearts of those who seek the Lord rejoice!

                                              (1 Chron. 16.7 – 10)

The joy of the people is supreme when, a generation later, the
Temple is finally built, and the ark comes to its final resting
place. Even the instruments were magnificent: 'lyres also and
harps for the singers; there never was seen the like of them
before in the land of Judah' (2 Chron. 9.11, 1 Kings 10.12).
At that great occasion, when all the singers and musicians
came to sing 'For he is good, for his steadfast love endures
forever', the temple was filled with the cloud of God's presence
in glory (2 Chron. 5.11 – 14).

The life of God's people was hardly limited to these high
moments of worship. Most of the time they worked, they
played, they loved and married. It is a mistake to think of this
as 'secular' life in any sense other than that it is not public
temple-worship. Since all was done 'to the glory of God' there
was no dichotomy. Music existed to accompany all these
other activities. The music was no less 'religious' than cult
music. It had other purposes, but it was no less oriented
toward God. The following sample of song species from the
Bible shows both the extensiveness of musical function and
the Godward commitment of the various forms.

Work songs (Num. 21.17 – 18; Isa. 16.10; 27.2; Jer. 25.30;
48.33; Hos. 2.17; Zech. 4.7).

Music connected with war, marching, and victory (Num.
21.27 – 30; Ps. 68; 2 Chron. 20.21; Num. 10.35 – 6; Exod.
15.20; Judg. 5.1; 1 Sam. 21.12; Ps. 24.7 – 10).

Songs for instruction, prophecy and mutual edification
(Deut. 3.19; 1 Kings 4.32; 2 Kings 3.15; 1 Chron. 25.1 – 3;
Col. 3.16).

Love songs, wedding music, songs of seduction (Ps. 45;
Song of Sol. 2.12; Ezek. 33.32; Isa. 5.1; Gen. 31.27; Jer.
25.10; 33.11; Isa. 23.15 – 16).

Entertainment (Job 21.12; Isa. 24.9; 2 Sam. 19.35; Lam.
5.14; Dan. 6.18; Amos 6.5).

Music with dance (Exod. 15.20; 32.18 – 19; 1 Sam. 18.6 – 7;
21.12; 29.5; Pss. 30.11 – 12; 68.25; 87.7; Matt. 11.17).

Songs of derision (Job 30.9; Lam. 3.14, 63; Isa. 14.4).

Mourning and lamentation (2 Sam. 1.18−27; 1 Kings 13.30; 2 Chron. 35.25; Ps. 69.12; Job 30.31; Eccles. 12.5; Jer. 9.16−17; 22.18; Ezek. 27.30−2).

A close examination of any of these references will reveal that in no case is the use of music neutral. It is religiously conditioned, either in covenant obedience or rebellion. Religion in Israel was not an irrational 'encounter with the sacred', which had to be cultivated through ritual and taboo systems. It was rather *life* under the covenant, life in relation to Jehovah. As such, there were no artificial boundaries between sacred and secular activities. To be sure, there were moments of heightened religious experience, such as when God appeared, or when the Temple was rebuilt. These called for special music (see e.g. Ezra 3.10−11). But then there were many more occasions when music was simply a part of life. If we follow up the references in the category I have called 'entertainment' we get a glimpse of the way music functioned in daily life. In 2 Samuel 19.35, Barzillai, an old man whom King David rewarded for his aid given at a difficult time, can hardly believe the kindness of the King: 'I am this day eighty years old; can I discern what is pleasant and what is not? Can your servant taste what he eats or what he drinks? *Can I still listen to the voice of singing men and singing women*? Why then should your servant be an added burden to my lord the king?' Music is part of life; like the enjoyment of food, it is a sign of health and vigour. In Job's complaint to Eliphaz we learn more about music in daily life (Job 21). Job deeply feels the injustice of his plight, which he compares to the prosperity of the wicked. Despite their rebellion against God, everything seems to go well for them. Their children grow up, their houses are safe, their cattle breed well, and

> They send forth their little ones like a flock,
>   and their children dance.
> They sing to the tambourine and the lyre,
>   and rejoice to the sound of the pipe (21.11−12).

In normal circumstances music is a sign of prosperity and peace. It does not seem just to Job that these particular people

49

should enjoy the privilege. Indeed many of the prophets carp against the pretentious use of music. 'Take away from me the noise of your songs,' says the Lord through Amos (5.23); 'to the melody of your harps I will not listen.' When judgement comes on a city, one of the signs of calamity is the absence of mirthful sounds. In a most striking metaphor, Isaiah announces the doom of Tyre by saying: 'The wine mourns, the vine languishes, all the merry-hearted sigh. The mirth of the timbrels is stilled, the noise of the jubilant has ceased, the mirth of the lyre is stilled' (Isa. 24.7 – 8).

Obviously music was not only the expression of joy. Music was heard on many different occasions in Israel, including mourning. But never is there a relegation of it to some sort of secular realm, where God's presence has no significance. God listens to the people's music, just as he watches over all of their life. Sometimes, as in Amos's times, music is used as a cover, as a shield against facing the truth. In that case it becomes 'noise': that kind of music should be stopped (see Jer. 25.10). There is a time to sing and dance (Song of Sol. 2.12). But there is also a time to refrain from dance (Eccles. 3.4). It all depends on the appropriateness of the circumstances. It all depends on the conditions of life under the covenant. The omnipresent background music of today fails to comply with this kind of orientation. What is particularly irritating about 'Muzak' is that one must be subjected to it regardless of the circumstance, and regardless of the opportunity. When a culture is deeply involved in decadence and autonomy, the pseudo-joyful sounds of a thousand strings is really blasphemy. This is not because of its secular character. It is because it does not faithfully reflect the distinctions entailed in covenant life.

So cultural life may not be artificially divided into sacred and secular. In the presence of God every part of life has religious significance. Not all occasions in life before Jehovah are characterized by the same intensity of religious experience. Not every part of the meal is a sweet! Music's function varies tremendously according to the occasion, according to social structure, according to time and place. We live in an age of rapid cultural change. Music reflects that. We also live in a compartmentalized world, reflected in our paradigms. The existence of 'highbrow' and 'lowbrow' music attests to that as

50

well. If music is a cultural category, it is bound to reflect social norms. But in the biblical ideal it is not 'sacred', nor is it Art with a capital 'A'. It is one aspect of the created order, in which, in a very real sense, everything is sacred!

In that sense, it is proper to say with the Psalmist, 'Singers and dancers alike say, "All my springs are in you"' (Ps. 87.7).

3: How Does Music Mean?

The odd-sounding title of this chapter is deliberate. From the previous pages we can see that neither cultural life in general nor music in particular can be neutral. As human covenant activity, music has its ultimate meaning in life as it is determined by the presence of God. This may be in harmony with him or in rebellious alienation. However, it is one thing to recognize that there is value in music, but quite another to discover how. How does music mean? Are there absolute norms for musical meaning? Can we discover criteria for good and bad music?

These are questions which have baffled the best minds over the centuries, and I make no pretence of having all the answers. Nevertheless certain aspects of the problem can be clarified within the theological perspective suggested in the previous chapter. We can at least avoid some of the major pitfalls.

Is There a Message?

Many people, including Evangelical Christians, are concerned to discover the message in the medium. It is common to find Christians who have been exposed to the exciting view that the Bible applies to every area of life looking for the 'world-view' behind a work of art before all else. There is a certain validity to this approach, as we shall see, but there are serious dangers. The most obvious is neglecting the art object. In the previous chapter I made a plea for keeping culture within a limited sphere, not to be confused with religious commitment. A work of art is not mainly a religious statement, although it may reflect religious engagement, as we shall try to explain. In evaluating such a work it is important first to approach it as art.

An added difficulty in dealing with music as a cultural phenomenon is that not all cultural activities are the same in nature. For example, kinship patterns in various societies relate to cultural life. So do women's fashions. Because culture is not neutral, as we have seen, we can find various ways in which kinship patterns and clothing styles reflect certain

52

world-views. The way a young British teenager may dress says something about adolescence in England. But it will be indirect, because of the relatively low symbolic value of fashion.

Music, on the other hand, is a cultural activity with relatively high symbolic value. At least it has a greater tie with symbolification than kinship and fashions. This means that the problem of meaning in music is a special one. Simply calling it a cultural activity does not say enough about its particular way of meaning as music.

In saying this, we are not necessarily coming into the camp of formalism. There is a strong tendency today to adopt the formalist view that art has no meaning outside itself. This is a perfectly understandable reaction to the simplistic view that art is merely a vehicle for a message. Aestheticians taking the formalist position insist that art-forms *mean* only in terms of themselves. Even literary prose, they say, should not be understood to be *about* persons and events, or even emotions, let alone ideas. The meaning of a text should be established not by studying the author's background, the period, the genre, etc., but the word-relationships and syntactical interplay. Structuralism is an advanced expression of this aesthetic. This school rejects the attribution of emotions, social function, psychological factors to literature. The meaning is contained within the contrasts, metaphors, oppositions, and dynamic features of the words and sentences.

In music formalism has many adherents. Pierre Boulez, the well-known French composer and conductor, has been a crusader for this view. His concern is to rid musical systems of every non-musical criterion. Numbers, pictures, psycho-physiological factors are beside the point. The point is to relate directly to the sound, without going through the grid of extra-musical factors. Traditionalism is our enemy because it makes us attribute banal meanings to sounds which are already meaningful within their relational features. We should be satisfied to enjoy music in the same way as we enjoy a mobile, with its fascinating balance and interplay of objects.[1]

While Boulez argues very cogently for his formalism, there is a flaw. All the time that he spends defending modern serialized music is also time spent defending modernity as such. Serial music, very much in vogue in the 1950s and 60s, conceives of musical form around the series, or tone-row, a group of twelve notes which determine the rest of the piece by their structural interrelationships. Boulez defends serialism because it is modern. Within his Hegelian view of history anyone who denies modernity is guilty of traditionalism. Instead, we must bend with evolutionary trends and accept today's 'musical universe'.[2] This is extramusical meaning! I am using this expression in the broadest sense. I recognize that not even Boulez claims that no relation exists at all between outside factors and musical meaning. If he did, he could not have written such pieces as *Rituel In Memoriam Maderna* (1974), for example. Yet Boulez claims that music does not reflect any kind of objective order, that it does not express anything in particular. He speaks forcefully against the idea that the composer writes in a way analogous to God's creation, carefully choosing the possibilities before him when he writes. And yet he also claims that we must submit to the irreversible mandate of history.[3] In a way, history has taken the place of the analogy of God that he rejects.

Igor Stravinsky was also a formalist. In his autobiography he discusses audience reactions to his *Symphony of Psalms*. One critic wrote that it was Hebrew in spirit, but lacked enough reminiscences of the synagogue. Stravinsky strongly objects to this sort of association. He complains that people always want to know what a piece expresses, and what the composer had in mind when writing it. 'They never seem to understand that music has an entity of its own apart from anything that it may suggest to them.' People who listen to music because it gives them emotions like joy, grief, sadness, an image of nature, and so on, are escaping. They want a drug! 'When people have learned to love music for itself, when they listen with other ears, their enjoyment will be of a far higher and more potent order, and they will be able to judge it on a higher plane and realize its intrinsic value.'[4]

I must say that I appreciate Stravinsky's concern, and Boulez' as well. It will not do to reduce music to some sort of message, a code-system which expresses something else. Stravinsky tries to protect music from invasions by well-intentioned listeners who do not seem to be able to grapple with a musical texture. His plea for an 'achieved order' is along these lines. But still, he goes too far. For him musical emotion is in no way connected with ordinary ones. For him the sensation is one of fascination with architectural forms.[5] *Emotion* and *fascination* still qualify as extra-musical no matter how we try to disconnect them from other things. A piece of music simply cannot be disconnected from other realms of experience. Stravinsky's music is a superb example of the connectedness. Think of titles like *The Rite of Spring*, and *In Memoriam Dylan Thomas*. The Stravinsky *Mass* is rich in historical connotation and religious feeling. To be sure there are structural features of Stravinsky's works which can occupy theoreticians for years. Much of modern music in the West is preoccupied with architectonic aspects and abstract formal relations. Much of it seems devoid of human feeling. Yet even the most abstract mathematical puzzle applied to sounds still attracts a certain fascination and provokes reflection which relate it to other parts of life.

The opposite of formalism is propaganda art. This is the view that art is merely a vehicle for ideals or emotions. Here the tendency is to minimize the formal features of a work and concentrate on ways of getting the message out. The problem with this is not that there is no relation, as the formalists maintain, but that the relation is not direct. Put another way, the coefficient between the music and extra-musical values is not always very high. The problem is rendered more complex because of the fact that much music has been written with the intention of provoking an effect in the listener. When this is done to the extent that the form is weakened, the music loses its value as a sovereign entity in the covenant world. That is to say, we may argue on aesthetic grounds that music ought not to be propaganda, but our aesthetics must recognize that some music is highly propagandist. In what follows, then, we are basically arguing for what should be, not for what is, although it is impossible to separate the two. In my opinion many discussions over the problem of meaning in the arts have failed to make this distinction, and as a result have been driven to make careless generalizations based on existing art, often western art, taking it as a sort of standard simply because it is there (or because many people, scholars, audiences, etc., approve of it), rather than determining standards from another source and applying them to the arts. Naturally standards cannot be developed in isolation from existing art. But it is hopeless to proceed by taking every possible example of art in the world, and then coming up with a theory that fits.

The Scripture is our ultimate norm. But God's word does not speak in an abstract way, since the author of that word is the same as the author of creation and human activity. There is complementarity between special revelation, what the Bible says, and general revelation, what we learn from the world. While the Scripture is ultimate authority, the created world also holds authority, so that it could be said that Scripture makes no sense apart from the sense of the world. What complicates matters is that we live in a fallen world. All is not right in the world, and that includes the world of music. Our aesthetic, in order to be fully biblical, must take into account the nature of creation, on the one hand, and the ambiguities of the fallen world, on the other. Ambiguous because man is in revolt against God, but at the same time God has not abandoned the world. There are evidences of his grace and care in every realm, including the arts.

In the issue of formalism and propaganda in art these considerations have a direct bearing. John Cage is a modern composer whose music has strong ties with his desire to convert western listeners to the world-view of Zen Buddhism. His music is quite openly meant to be propaganda for that view. His convictions about Zen Buddhism led him to revise all traditions within European music, including the idea that individual will is involved in the composing process. In 1952 he decided to break with tradition by writing *4'33''*. In this work a solo pianist comes out to play, but closes the lid of the piano and remains silent for four minutes and thirty-three seconds. The only 'sounds' are from the environment, or those made by the audience. Cage's principle is to make compositions 'free of individual taste and memory in their order of events', and to 'let sounds be themselves in a space of time'.[6] Cage has devoted his life to communicating the Zen message of purposelessness. His music is meant to be free from human intervention. By listening to it audiences may be 'converted' to this view. Musically, the result is an almost total absence of form.

Does this mean that Cage's music has no meaning? That question shows us another important feature of the problem of music's meaning. In terms of his philosophy of Zen Buddhism, Cage's music has meaning. It is in fact a vehicle for his views, since listeners subjecting themselves to silence from a piano enter into the mentality of Zen. Yet in relation to the real world that God has created, the music is meaningful as rebellion against the truth. Furthermore, by attempting to remove all formal elements the composer is going against the grain of the nature of man as image-bearer of God. But there is more at stake than simply a well-communicated world-view. Musically, the result is a kind of reduction of everything to elements whose only function is to 'say something'. The music becomes thin, serving more as a vehicle for a message than as musical texture with its own volume and strength.

The meaning of the art object is brought out by the formal structure. For example, we could ask how do the blues convey meaning? Many things could be said, because the genre is rich. But one feature of the blues is its simple A-A-B structure. Most of the time the first A is in the tonic of the key. The second A is in the sub-dominant (that would be the F triad in the key of C). The B section begins in the dominant (G in the key of C), and then back to tonic. Of course many elements come in to flesh out this bare structure. Often notes are bent and tensions are created with the use of 'blue notes' like the flatted third and seventh. While there is an almost infinite variety of blues, the rhythm is often a forward-propelling 'swinging' beat, so characteristic of all black American music. Now, this A-A-B structure is paralleled by the words, which make a simple statement twice, and then either resolve it or present some sort of conclusion in the third phrase. Here are the first stanzas of Charley Patton's 'Bird Nest Bound'.

Come, on mama, out to the edge of town
Come, on mama, go to the edge of town
I know where there's a bird nest, built down on the ground.

If I was a bird, mama . . . [the two guitars finish the line]
If I was a bird, mama, I would find a nest in the heart of town
(*Spoken*:) Lord, you know I'd build it in the heart of town
So when the town get lonesome, I'd be bird nest bound.

57

> Hard luck is at your front door, blues are in your room
> Hard luck is at your front door, blues are in your room
> Callin' at your back door, what is gonna become of you?[7]

There are many fascinating aspects to this blues which we could go into. What is of interest, however, is the structure of the two statements, the A and B. Notice how the final phrase brings the idea of the first statement forward. It may do it by asserting with confidence that there is an answer. It may explain why something is needed. It may even raise another question. The important feature to see is the bringing forward to another plane. This is why the blues have been called optimistic, despite the narrow definition of the term. There *are* sad blues, but there are blues about almost every subject conceivable. Yet the underlying structure communicates *resolution*, at least at some level, of a problem.

The music of the blues is perfectly fitted for this way of meaning. It is not just the sequence tonic/sub-dominant/dominant/tonic which lends itself to the feeling of resolution, but the distribution of these harmonies within the metrical structure, usually of twelve bars (measures). And there is much more . . . but the form is pregnant with meaning.

Is it a Language?
In the blues a close connection exists between the text and the musical form. For many people music is a language, or at least language seems to be the perfect metaphor for music. It is often said that 'music is a universal language'. Superficially, Scripture would seem to justify this assertion. The close connection of words and music in the Bible is amply attested. The trouble comes when we try to apply the analogy to specific cases.

The first notion that must be challenged is the universality of the 'language' of music. When an audience sits through a marvellous performance of Beethoven's *Eroica Symphony* it is tempting to feel that there is a kind of communion going on. Barriers are thus broken down by a common experience of great music. In the same way when Benny Goodman played jazz in Moscow, he was called America's 'musical ambassador behind the iron curtain'. What years of negotiations could not accomplish, music could. But the analogy with language is not very solid. Presumably the Muscovites enjoyed the sounds produced from the Goodman orchestra, so that in a sense they 'agreed' that this music was good. In that sense there was communication. But communication in art is not the same as communication in language. At the negotiating table the language used (and translated) fails to provide good feeling and agreement not because it is verbal as opposed to musical, but because it *does* communicate. It communicates content that cannot be agreed upon. The disagreement comes not because people on either side of the negotiating table cannot enjoy the language used, but because they have different views, different economic policies, etc. Now language cannot change people's ideologies. It may help clarify issues. Understanding how to use certain terms, to introduce certain logical sequences, may help as well. But the function of language as such is not to promote agreement.

Benny Goodman's jazz gave pleasure in Moscow because it is warm, because it swings, because of a hundred features of the 'Swing' style. The Russians agreed about the virtues of the music, not about western ideology. What if America had sent Navajo Indians to perform tribal ritual music instead of Benny Goodman? Would that have been equally appreciated? What if the Muscovites had been subjected to Inuit Eskimo 'throat-game music'? Certainly the reaction would have been bewilderment or even anger. There is no universality here. Eskimo music is very hard for Westerners to understand. Only after years of study and contact with Eskimo culture can the music be appreciated by Westerners, and then, possibly, enjoyed. In contrast to this the big band sound is very close to the kind of music the Russians, and other Westerners from a certain social background, are used to hearing. This leaves us with a very weakened form of the analogy. It might be safe to say that certain styles, like languages, are better understood by members of two different parts of the world than others. But then we are not saying very much.

We shall do better if we restrict our investigations to some more modest claims about music and language. Many people have analysed musical structure *in terms of* linguistic structure. That is, they have found analogies between phonological or grammatical features of a language and

59

elements in the musical texture. One may speak of phrases, periods, sentences, etc., in the classical sonata, for example. This parallel is further aided because certain musical traditions are clearly derived from vocal influence. The blues is a case in point. But so is South Indian instrumental music. Modern Indian performance practice reflects the characteristic textual features of later Sanskrit poetry and of the 'medieval' and modern vernaculars in at least three ways.[8] First, the poems are characterised by refrain and stanza design, unlike the older poetry in which every quatrain is an independent entity. This is paralleled in the music by the contrast between a fundamental part with its register and thematic content, and a second, responding part in a different register. Second, the poems are in *rondeau* form both semantically and grammatically. The last words of the stanza are continued and completed logically in the beginning of the independent refrain. In the music there are linear connections at the boundaries from each register into the next, creating a kind of musical lead-back from the endings of the two parts to the beginning of the principle part. And third, there is usually a matching rhyme of stanzas with refrain, or even matching words, which ensures a natural flow back to the beginning. In the music there is 'rhyme' as well in that the melodies are the same or very close.

There is no doubt that musical meaning is closely bound to linguistic considerations in cases like the blues and Indian classical music. But there are two problems connected with the analogy that must be understood if it is not to lead us too far astray into sweeping generalizations about music as language. First, not all musics are so closely dependent on language, formally, as the cases before us. Harold Powers, who is one of the world experts on Indian music, has this to say:

> Until a few years ago I took it for granted that I would find it easy enough to show that the parallels between music and language are as close and as deep elsewhere as they are for Indian classical music. But in recent years work with non-Indian Asian musics, and in the history of European music theory, has led me to think that the striking validity of the language-music analogy in Indian classical music is probably far from typical. It is not, though, that

other musics are in no way formally like language. It is rather that few musics are as much like language as Indian music is.[9]

The first problem, then, is that the direct connection between text and music is not the same from genre to genre.

The second problem is that there are a number of ways in which music is quite unlike language. For example, all human languages are apparently characterized by much the same degree of complexity. 'Linguistically' there is great similarity from one language to another, despite certain differences in the structure of various languages. This is not true of different musical systems, which vary a great deal in complexity, or density, from one genre to another. This is the case not only of the 'amount' of density, but of the *kind* of musical texture as well. A comparison between two languages will not reveal the same differences as a comparison between, say Gregorian chant and a five-voice fugue. The chant is close to language in that it is in unison, unaccompanied. But the comparison with the complex polyphony of a fugue, where several voices are interwoven, 'speaking' different sentences in chorus cannot be made with language. It is far better to compare complex ensemble music from one culture to another rather than comparing both to the external model of language.

Elaborate attempts have been made to develop *a certain kind* of linguistic model for music. For example, generative grammar has been used to try and explain different melodic types. Many theorists who are enthusiastic about finding the 'deep-structures' which underlie the surface in language have rushed in to apply the concept to music. While some fascinating work has been done, the pitfalls are many. For example, Leonard Bernstein's famous 1973 Norton Lectures at Harvard, entitled *The Unanswered Question*, were a bold attempt at finding surface manifestations of deep-structures in every kind of music. Beginning with Noam Chomsky's linguistic theories, he described what he believed to be a worldwide musical grammar. Certain elements like the recurrence of the note-relationship—E, C, D sharp, C sharp—in Bach, Stravinsky and even Hindu music, put him on the trail. A convinced evolutionist, Bernstein traced the origin of music to the sound 'Ma', which is almost universally the word for mother. The road from this 'primal scream' to music was long but irreversible. Bernstein shows that many children's songs build on the minor third ('rain, rain, go away'), and that various primitive music systems use the pentatonic scale (black notes on our keyboard).

The errors in the evolutionary theory of music, and the corollaries in such supposedly universal patterns as the minor third have been denounced, and for the most part the hypothesis of diffusionism (a common origin for musical traits), at least in its simplistic forms, has been discarded. It turns out that most of these note-relationships don't really exist in many different cultures after all.[10] Furthermore, there are many problems connected with the deep-structure/surface-structure model as applied to music. The 'deeper' one goes — and one must go deep because the surface is so diversified — the further we are from real music, and the real world, for that matter.[11] Bernstein is aware of this. But he attributes the distance to artistic creativity!

> What is really being clarified here, I hope, is a new kind of ambiguity — a structural ambiguity . . . The surface structure we have just been examining is dramatically at variance with (the) deep structure which we investigated earlier . . . These ambiguities, I must emphasize, are beautiful and are germane to all artistic creation. They enrich our aesthetic response . . . by providing more than one way of perceiving the aesthetic surface.[12]

This is very revealing. Could it be that Bernstein, while not renouncing his linguistic model, is redirecting the enquiry toward a more human source? Could it be that he senses the abstract nature of the language analogy, at least in its Chomskian form, and opts for a more creative beginning place? In his concluding Norton Lecture, he referred to 1966 as a musical low-point in our century. Atonal music and doctrinaire serialism reigned. Even Stravinsky was 'converted' to serialism. Then, when he died, in 1971, young composers were free. They fell back on their own, innate responses, and music once again stood a chance of being qualified as *poetry.*

Here we have the crux of the matter. The problem with the language analogy to music is not that there is no validity to it. Many useful parallels can be found, and our understanding of musical forms can be enriched by comparisons with language. The difficulty is with an *abstract* view of language, one that does not deal with it as human. Language cannot be divorced from humankind as image of God. Human language is a rich of repository of genres, statements, feelings. It is one of the primary vehicles for relating to God as well as to other people. This is what Bernstein is groping after, even though he does not seem to have the ultimate framework which would allow him confidently to assert that human creativity is more than a bridge between deep and surface structures. What he qualifies as 'ambiguity' we would call 'covenant response'. The role of human beings is central both in creativity and in language-using. Because it is human to be both creative and language-using it is no wonder that we find so many analogies between music, which orders sounds within a time scheme, and language, which similarly orders words and phrases. There is analogy, but not identity. Music is not 'a language'. It has a very different function. Music is not even primarily a way to 'heighten' language. It is true that when music accompanies a text, there is a close-knit interrelationship between the two, or at least there should be. Music can indeed 'bring out' certain values in the words. It is one thing to say the words, 'O God, our help in ages past, our hope for years to come'. It is another thing to sing them to the majestic hymn by William Croft, with its succession of half-notes in step-by-step chord changes in the key of B flat. The music is appropriate. It is fitting. But it cannot be reduced somehow to the words. Nor are the words merely a 'text' to be 'set' to the music. What is happening instead is that the music projects a world which the words do as well, but in a very different modality. If we hear the music alone, and had no idea it was the setting for an Isaac Watts hymn, we would surely not be able to guess the subject. We might be able to say that the music had a certain solemnity, a certain majesty. These notions are, of course, culture-specific. An aboriginal tribesman would not even be able to say that much about it. But a Westerner would. Yet he would have no idea of the theme in the words. The music only 'heightens' the words because a third force is at work when the two are brought together. The hymn is both musical and linguistic, and a complex relationship is established between the two. In a way, we could even say that the words 'heighten' the music. Why not? At any rate, the final product is its own, integrated

63

work of art, whose purpose is to fit into one particular dimension of human existence, public worship. The meaning of this final product is in terms of its 'fittingness' to public worship.[13]

So music is indeed connected with the way we speak. But it is also connected with the way we breathe, the way we run, the way we cook. In other words, while there are particular affinities with speech, there are many other parallels. This all underlines what was said in the previous chapter. Music is a sphere in its own right, however closely related it may be to other spheres. This view is certainly the biblical one. Music is more than a secondary language. It has its own reality, and its own way of meaning. The meaning can (and must) be described in words. But it cannot be reduced to some sort of verbal analogy.

Still, my hope is that we will continue to find linguistic analogies and models for musical analysis. If we do not make them a substitute, nor hope for too much from them, they can be useful in understanding how music means. Perhaps we could best conclude with Harold Powers:

> Musical scholars may well and profitably look to linguistics for suggestive notions, but the differences between music and language are great, and the special difficulties of working with music greater still, and no amount of even genuine sophistication and experience in linguistics can serve a musical scholar as substitute for an informed awareness of both the methods and the matter of musical studies themselves.[14]

What About Emotions?

Almost every culture, from the ancients to modern people, agrees that whatever else it can mean, music means emotion. A number of intellectual traditions from the great civilizations connect music with emotions in specific ways. It is most often at the level of 'art music' rather than popular or folk music that a relation is seen. Different scales or modes were believed to influence our emotions, and various systems of classification were proposed in order to assign specific emotional results from specific musical influences. According to Aristotle, the ancient Greek philosophers believed that there were three types of melodies linked to three extra-musical realities. The 'ethical' melodies could relax the soul, 'practical' melodies helped with incentive to work, and 'enthusiastic' melodies (always in the Phrygian mode, probably a pentatonic scale) led to dionysiac emotional excitement. Since the ancient Greeks there have been many ways of explaining the emotional power of music, some not at all plausible for modern people. What is striking, however, is the great consensus that exists in favour of believing there is a connection. Today it is the same. Hardly anyone will deny the reality of music's emotional impact. Many people speak of sad pieces, happy songs, moving symphonies, and so on.

The Bible is in accord with this consensus. Of the more than six hundred references to music in the Scriptures, the great majority connect it with some kind of emotional experience. The natural passage of thought between feelings and sounds is most remarkable. In Isaiah the return of God's people to the Promised Land is described in terms of deep joy: 'And the ransomed of the Lord shall return, and come to Zion with singing; everlasting joy shall be on their heads' (35.10; 51.11).

Jeremiah speaks of 'the voice of mirth, the voice of gladness, the voice of the bridegroom, the voice of the bride' (16.9; 25.10). The 'voice of' is a frequent biblical formula to express music in its relation to emotions. Psalm 98 is a fine example of the interplay of joy and the voice of melody (translated 'sound' most frequently):

Make a joyful noise to the Lord, all the earth;
    break forth into joyous song and sing praises!
Sing praises to the Lord with the lyre,
    with the lyre and the *sound of melody*!
With trumpets and the *sound of the horn*,
    make a joyful noise before the King, the Lord! (vv. 4—6)

The instruments themselves are able to convey joy (see Ps. 45.8; 71.22; 92.1—4). Thus musical instruments are not only appendages to words that speak of joy, but they have their own way of meaning. This is the reason why the Bible writers often separate vocal praise from melody, even though they be simultaneous. The Christians at Ephesus are told to address one another 'in psalms and hymns and spiritual songs, singing *and* making melody to the Lord with all your

65

heart' (Eph. 5.19). Psalm 149 alludes to dancing and music-making without a specific connection to words:

Let Israel be glad in his Maker,
　let the sons of Zion rejoice in their King!
Let them praise his name with dancing,
　making melody to him with timbrel and lyre. (vv. 2, 3)

Sometimes in the Bible the instruments themselves are personified in terms of emotional values. A lyre may be sweet (Ps. 81.2); the harp and lyre may be roused from slumber (Pss. 57.8; 108.2). When Jacob fled secretly from his unjust employer Laban, what he missed, according to his indignant father-in-law, was joyful music: 'I might have sent you away with mirth and songs, with tambourine and lyre' (Gen. 31.27).

Joy is not the only emotion music can express, according to Scripture. It is true that music is a particularly appropriate way of experiencing gladness (see Jas. 5.13). It is also true that imposing mirthful songs on a depressed person is tactless (Prov. 25.20). But there are mournful harps which can 'turn to the *voice of weeping*'. Lamentation is often expressed in music (2 Sam. 1.18–27; Job 30.31; Jer. 31.15; 48.36; Matt. 9.23). In one fascinating passage, there seems to be music of two kinds, one joyful and the other mournful. In this case 'the people could not distinguish the sound of the joyful shout from the sound of the people's weeping' (Ezra 3.13).

While it is clearly correct to find this close association between music and the emotions, what is less clear is how the relationship works. How does music express emotions? Surely it is not simply a matter of producing a pleasurable sensation. There may be such feelings of pleasure evoked by a certain timbre, or combination of sounds, but that is extremely limited. The psychologist Leonard Meyer denounces three errors which he says have plagued the psychology of music since its beginnings, *hedonism*, *atomism*, and *universalism*.[15] Hedonism is the confusion of aesthetic experience with the sensuously pleasing. It is what I would call the 'I like it' syndrome. The emotions of joy and mournfulness, for example, would be connected with pleasure and displeasure, according to this theory, and that is clearly very far from what these emotions mean. Atomism is related. It seeks the key to emotion in music in the succession of separable sound complexes. Universalism goes a step further and says that people from any background will have the same sensation. These three errors, which are really the same, are rooted in the false approach which tries to derive musical experience from physical or acoustical features alone. Furthermore, says Meyer, music theory has fallen prey to these same errors:

> Attempts to explain the effect of the minor mode of western music, to cite but one example, in terms of consonance and dissonance or in terms of the harmonic series have resulted in uncontrolled speculations and untenable theories. Even those not thus haunted by the ghost of Pythagoras have contributed little to our understanding of musical meaning and its communication. For, on the whole, music theorists have concerned themselves with the grammar and syntax of music rather than with its meaning or the affective experiences to which it gives rise.[16]

Unfortunately Meyer himself falls into a particular variety of psycho-acoustical theory which relates musical experience to behavioural learning theory combined with *gestalt* psychology. According to this theory, patterns of continuity and discontinuity, tension and release, form the inner structure of the piece of music, and these correspond with our perception. The best music follows a pattern of a musical impulse toward a certain goal, then a resistance or delay, and then back to the goal.[17] This may be true for some pieces, as far as it goes, but it tends to reduce both music and emotion to stimuli and responses of a narrow sort. What Meyer does help with is relating meaning in music to experienced listening. In other words, his laws of tension and release are learned behaviour within definite cultural contexts. This is why, for example, when Westerners hear Arabic music for the first time, they are unable to listen to it meaningfully, although it is intended to be highly charged with emotional content. I believe the same would be true if Westerners, even believing Christians, listened to Old Testament music, the kind that Moses and David rejoiced by: they would derive almost no meaning from it. Musical patterns must be experienced 'from within' if they are to make sense, or communicate emotional values.

Another difficulty with Meyer's view is that it tends to isolate emotional response to the individual psychology rather than see it in a larger context. This is the standard way to

67

approach the arts in the rationalist philosophy stemming from the Enlightenment. According to the famous *Encyclopédie*, 'beauty' is derived from nature. It is then perceived by individual persons, who are also possessors of 'human nature'. Diderot said that music was superior to the other arts because, being perceived directly, without mediation, the imagination is left free. Art for him, and for the later Romantics as well, was not so much an imitation of nature but a source of 'pleasures of the imagination'.[18] There is no place in this thinking for the social function of art, nor for its analogy with other cultural activities.

Emotional response to music, like emotional life itself, is related to the broader horizon of social and cultural life. Even in the Bible the emotional value of music is deeply rooted in the experience of the people of God. That experience was strongly influenced by their situation in the history of redemption. When the New Testament writers exhort believers to sing psalms and hymns 'with thankfulness in your hearts to God' a specific connection is made between the singing, the emotion and the relationship to God (see Col. 3.16). Moreover, the setting is that of the Christian community, who must teach and mutually admonish through the word of Christ. Feelings expressed through music are never derived solely from the structure of the music, but from the context in which it is used:

> My lips will shout for joy,
>   when I sing praises to thee;
>   my soul also, which thou hast rescued.
> And my tongue will talk of thy righteous help
>   all the day long,
> For they have been put to shame and disgraced
>   who sought to do me hurt. (Ps. 71.23−4)

The man whose life has been saved by God responds, with patterned sounds, in the joy of thankfulness. This is more than pleasurable sensation. It places the emotional meaning of music, or rather its way of meaning, in the context of the covenant. To be sure, his heart is renewed by God's grace. The individual is not swallowed up in the social and cultural context. He can sing a 'new song' because he is a 'new person' in Christ.

The central message of biblical revelation is that God dwells with his people. This is the heart of the covenant: 'I will be your God and you shall be my people.' This is the good *news* of the gospel, new because salvation could never be accomplished by human means. The King of Kings tells John on Patmos, 'Behold, I make all things new' (Rev. 21.5). And so it is time for the 'new song' (Pss. 33.3; 40.3; 96.1; 98.1; 144.9; 149.1; Isa. 42.10; Rev. 5.9; 14.3). Old songs will not do. When God accomplishes his work of salvation, his people respond with the deepest kind of joyful song. This was true for Moses, Deborah, Miriam and David in the Old Testament. It is true of believers in the New Testament (Rev. 15.3).

Not that the Bible encourages mindless abandon. Believers are told to sing with their understanding (1 Cor. 14.15; cf. Ps. 47.7). But the emotional content of music is tied in both with that intelligent response and with its ultimate cause. And it can also be rebellion against that ultimate source, producing the 'noise of your songs' (Amos 5.23). The response of human beings to God's revelation may well be negative, making the emotional content of the music quite different. The contrast between the two expressions is sharply made in Psalm 137, a song of exile in Babylon:

> On the willows there
> we hung up our lyres.
> For there our captors
> required of us songs,
> and our tormentors, mirth, saying,
> 'Sing us one of the songs of Zion!'
> How shall we sing the Lord's song
> in a foreign land? (vv. 2—4)

How indeed can the emotional content expressing the faith of the covenant people be sung in a context where God has unleashed the chastisements of the covenant-curse (Deut. 29.16—28)? They will have to wait for the day of restoration in order to resume their thankful music. And as it happens, God promises just that through the prophet Jeremiah:

Thus says the Lord: In this place of which you say, 'It is a waste without man or beast,' in the cities of Judah and the streets of

69

Jerusalem that are desolate, without man or inhabitant or beast, there shall be heard again the voice of mirth and the voice of gladness, the voice of the bridegroom and the voice of the bride, the voice of those who sing, as they bring thank offerings to the house of the Lord . . . For I will restore the fortunes of the land as at first, says the Lord. (Jer. 33.10−11)

Emotional meaning is not primarily a function of the construction of the composition in isolation from other factors. It is a function of the sign-value of the piece. Just as a certain football cheer means victory, and our national anthems mean patriotic fervour, biblical song is a function of a *metaphorical* impact. It goes far deeper than a 'signal'. The red light 'signals' the traffic to stop. But the musical metaphor is richer. It depends on a whole network of significations.[19]

Here we are close to the heart of the matter. Like myth (in its truest sense) music has heuristic value. In an artistic way it tells us something specific, concrete, musically valid, about reality. And it organizes it into a creative unit which ensures that it does more than just represent the artist's mood of the moment. Susanne K. Langer believes that the essence of the way to express emotional life is in the musical realm, and specifically in the rhythmical factor of musical composition:

Vital organization is the frame of all feeling, because feeling exists only in living organisms; and the logic of all symbols that can express feeling is the logic of organic processes. The most characteristic principle of vital activity is rhythm. All life is rhythmic . . . This rhythmic character of organism permeates music, because music is a symbolic presentation of the highest organic response, the emotional life of human beings . . . The great office of music is to organize our conception of feeling into more than an occasional awareness of emotional storm, i.e. to give us an insight into what may truly be called the 'life of feeling', or subjective unity of experience.[20]

Being a subjective unity of experience does not mean that the cause of emotion is necessarily in the individual. Performers around the world whose music has an emotional impact depend on many factors in order to succeed. They create a 'world' by using all the stylistic and conventional means at their disposal. The effect of producing emotional reactions

70

can only take place if the elements that make up that world are accepted. Acceptance depends on various factors as well. In some cultures the performer must follow strict rules handed down from the fathers in order to have the desired effect. They may be helping to construct a shared emotional impression for the community by the use of encoded signs such as a specific melody, a combination of instruments, accompaniment by dance, make-up, masks, and so on.[21]

Music's relation to emotion is not so much a matter of the physical properties of the sounds touching our own psychophysiological natures. The meaning of music for emotion is not primarily in its acoustical properties isolated from the symbolic presentation. Of course various types of music seek to affect us through such means as heavy drumming, loudness and amplification, etc. But the effects of these depend not so much on some biological process unleashed within the human organism as on deeper psychological factors. Music is movement. It is closely associated with human experience in space and time. Often related to the dance, music has the ability to 'move' me, to qualify my sense of being in the personal and corporate space in which I live. Its temporal architecture gives me an experience of time which is heightened and intensified. This is why a drum-roll at a circus tells me I am about to witness a spectacular jump from the trapeze. This is also why composers like John Williams know exactly when to use high-pitched violins to accompany a frightening scene in a movie. In the same way an organ prelude tells me I must prepare for worship. The way music *means*, emotionally, is primarily musical. It is through the many devices in the 'world' created by knowing use of many different compositional elements (which vary greatly from culture to culture) that emotional responses are produced.

This is why it is a mistake, for example, simply to equate the minor scale with sad or dark feelings and the major scale with joyful ones. The minor mode *alone* does not create a mood. It is through the use of the minor in combination with other factors that darker emotions can be aroused in western listeners. Beethoven's 'Funeral March', the second movement of his *Third Symphony* (1804), makes full use of the conventional tools at the composer's disposal to communicate heroic tragedy. The principal theme evokes the structure of

71

several funeral themes, without being identical with any of them. The slow deliberate pace of most of the movement brings us into the architectural space of dirge and lament. The oboe solos are 'lonely', the fugal sections are 'passionate', the sequence of agitation and calm recreate the human experience of struggle and rest. All of this is set in the minor mode, with occasional 'relief' in the major, thus, as we said, the minor mode alone does not create a mood, but the minor mode is not alone. Neither are any of the other compositional factors.

The individual factors indeed have no meaning in themselves! The 'life of feeling' that music can give us is only possible in a 'world of meaning.' This is God's world. Meaning is grounded in the structure of the created world because he is the Origin. Thus the *principle* of music's emotional signifying quality is not in such and such a sound or effect, but in the total architecture as it relates to human experience in the created world.

Music as Cultural Metaphor

The meaning of music depends on the meaning of meaning! This puts the issue on a higher level than simply the question of whether music *refers* to something outside itself. Reference is, of course, an important way of meaning. We may speak of the meaning of a word in these terms: to what does it refer? It is true that music can and does refer to things in the natural world. Couperin wrote a harpsichord piece that imitates the sound of a cuckoo bird. Peter's lament in the recitative setting of the biblical phrase 'he went out and wept bitterly' in Bach's *St John Passion* is, among other things, a physical imitation of a man crying. Programme music seeks to refer to extra-musical reality in a more subtle way. Berlioz' *Symphonie Fantastique* means to describe the experiences of a young man under the influence of a drug. This is a step above mere sound effects, but it still limits the meaning of the piece to a reference. In the well-known baroque doctrine of the 'musical affections' various conventions were established to ensure a connection between each emotion and a specific musical practice. Writers like Johann Mattheson described the emotions in terms of a limited number of psychological triggers, and then suggested corresponding musical devices.[22]

It is unclear whether the doctrine of the '*affekt*' involves the meaning of a piece or its effects. In any case, this too is a primary sort of reference.

Nevertheless the essential meaning of music is far more than this sort of correspondence. The formalists are right to insist that music has its own way of meaning. But they tend to ignore the larger context of meaning itself. We are in a sort of crisis of meaning today, as a brief look at the prevailing philosophical views will tell. Structuralism, like many other modern language philosophies, is in a perpetual search for meaning and value behind the words that evoke them. Where is the sense? Is it in the structural interrelationships of the words? In the oppositions and complements between phrases? As one reads such philosophical discussions one is under the impression of being completely lost in the particulars, of not being able to stand above to see the universals. It is rather like trying to discover the meaning of a beautiful vase by smashing it to pieces and examining each bit in the hope that it may reveal something essential. In formalist circles in music analysis it is the same. Boulez, Stockhausen and others seem to be lost in a labyrinth of particulars, with numbers studies, synthesized sounds and electronics of all kinds brought in for greater scrutiny of the details. But the meaning is 'from above', not 'from below', if the biblical framework is right.

Because our world is God's creation things have meaning both in a universal and in a particular way. We are not obliged to choose. When we look at a Cézanne still life, say a table with fruit on it, we see individual apples, oranges, and so on. But we see more. There is a universal quality which makes it more than just any fruit bowl with food. The artist sees the lines and dynamic forces which structure this group of components into a whole, into something greater than the sum of its parts. Not that the abstract quality of the universal swallows up the particular. Both sides of the equation remain persuasively real. This kind of meaning-structure is only possible in a world where God is the point of origin. Human beings can give meaning to the parts of the world because they are in God's image. Adam could *name* the animals, in Genesis 2, because of this meaning-structure. He not only called them something, or likened them to something outside

73

of themselves (as Bob Dylan's song suggests[23]), but he conferred sense on them, including their place in the created order, and their particular relation to mankind. This is the significance of the statement: 'The man gave names to all cattle, and to the birds of the air, and to every beast of the field; but for the man there was not found a helper fit for him' (Gen. 2.20). In the same way, music is a kind of 'naming'. It is a way of articulating human experience.[24] It can be articulate because in God's world there is a unity of experience which is not reduced but rather incarnated by the particulars.

Put another way, we live in a world where analogies are valid because of the unity stemming from the point of origin. Music, as we have seen, has *heuristic* value in exploring our God-created world. It is a kind of sound-adventure which, like the doing of a puzzle, allows us in a *musical way* to articulate the meaning of our creaturehood. In this way it has a similar function to that of the myth in Aristotle's terms. For him myth is not a simple copy, but a re-description. The myth takes a less-known entity, say human reality, and seeks to get closer to it by means of better-known entities like tragic fables or dramatic epics. Biblical revelation constantly uses signs, symbols, types, and other metaphorical devices to get us closer to the truth. Jeremiah broke ceramic vessels, Moses lifted a serpent onto a rod, Jesus healed a blind man. In addition to the immediate value of these actions, they have a heuristic function as well, leading us to discover a deeper truth about judgement and mercy. Music has this kind of metaphorical way of meaning. Metaphors operate at many levels. Sometimes they are narrow 'signals'. In music we know how certain sounds can 'trigger' a response because the associational value is strong. The national anthem, a favourite hymn, a school song, or even the bugle-call are examples of this direct kind of signal. On the other side, the metaphor may be quite indirect, even difficult to describe. In fact, musical description is a famous problem.

Perhaps it is best to begin modestly, not trying to lay bare the creative process in an effort to reduce it to words. But certain connections do exist, and surely it should be possible to work toward methods of study (and listening!) which uncover some of the basic links between the music metaphor and the created world of experience. In any case, some of the

74

pitfalls can be pointed out already. One is reducing the tools of analysis to one or two. For example, it is very common to centre all of the discussion of music from a certain period on *style*. First of all, this is a slippery concept. What is style? The best is to tie it in with certain particular practices, and to view it, 'not as something whole but as a collection of conventions, relatively uniform in the bulk of the music of a given period and idiosyncratically altered but nonetheless present in even its most original composers.'[25] In tandem with this, it is crucial to try to relate these conventions to the social and cultural settings in which the music is played. Ethnomusicology has begun to explore these dimensions, and some ground has been gained. Unfortunately its research is often cramped by the limited concepts of culture and society underlying the work. For example, culture may be used as a reductive notion, and include language and even religious commitment. Thus music would have to bear too much weight in terms of its meaning.

This brings us to the question of a world-view expressed in music. Can art in general and music in particular convey a particular philosophy of life, a world-view? If we agree with the metaphorical function of music, we can give a cautious 'yes' to that question. However, it is important to respect the distance between world-view and cultural expression in the order of human experience. And even at that, a world-view is more like a paradigm than essential religious commitment. The difference is that a paradigm is a way of structuring one's view of reality, of the cosmos. It is, of course, very much related to religious commitment, but it is not the same thing. I can be a Christian, because in my heart I have bowed to God as Creator and Redeemer through Jesus Christ, yet at the same time be espousing a Newtonian view of the universe, with notions such as mass, inertia, and the conservation of energy. Or I can espouse a more Einsteinian view of a space-time continuum. I can be a pessimist or an optimist about history, while still being a Christian. Music relates to my world-view by way of paradigms. This is why styles are so different from one group of people to another. The musical conventions and languages reflect different ways of structuring aesthetic experience, which in turn are understood as paradigms of thought. Furthermore, there will be reciprocal

75

relationships with music and social structure as well. The practice of music-making cannot be divorced from the way we live socially.

This gives rise to a much more dynamic concept of music's place in human experience. If we wanted to illustrate, it might look like the diagram below.

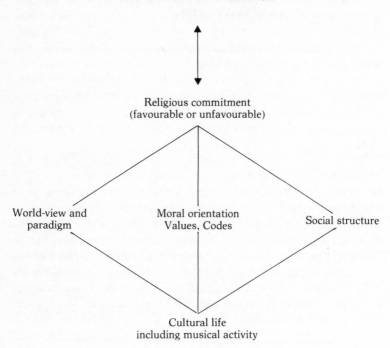

God's covenant revelation

Religious commitment
(favourable or unfavourable)

World-view and
paradigm

Moral orientation
Values, Codes

Social structure

Cultural life
including musical activity

The various components of human experience are ordered in a particular series of relationships. In the ultimate case everything depends on the primary religious commitment to the revelation of God, whether favourably or unfavourably disposed toward it. There could be an ambiguity here as well, since in most societies there is no clear consensus. Cultural life, including musical activity, is not directly related to religious commitment. It is dependent on three other factors which are more directly related to revelation: world-view,

76

moral values and social structure. For this reason it is impossible to divorce musical styles from these three entities. So it is that being a committed Christian, for example, does not mean that one's musical composition will be able to speak forth a Christian point of view, while by-passing the other realities. Musical meaning is filtered through paradigms, which are thought-categories and models that depend on many factors. It is filtered through moral codes and social structures as well. In fact cultural activity is itself full of conventions whose relationship to a world-view is not always obvious. This is in no way meant to discourage us from seeking such meanings as they relate to religious commitments. But the road is not easy to follow.

The *Mass in B minor* by Johann Sebastian Bach is undoubtedly a reflection of the composer's Orthodox Lutheran views. But in order to appreciate how, we must remember that he used many conventions which even his eighteenth-century audience may not have grasped, let alone ourselves. The key of B minor had special significance for Bach. The rich musical symbolism in many of the sections escapes us. Of course, we can feel certain things. The weight of the successive triads in descending pattern which Bach used to set the words 'Et incarnatus est' still speaks powerfully to us today. But we should be careful not to jump too fast to the conclusion that Bach was a sort of preacher who used music.

Music is like architecture in that sense. Some buildings are almost purely functional, like a hospital. Others combine function with symbolical values: churches, palaces, skyscrapers. Residential homes have a very special role, and so their dispositions are often organically related to the way people choose to live, to their habits, their pleasures, and so on. Most important, each of these kinds of buildings varies tremendously in style according to geographical, cultural and social norms. Music is the same. Some of it is narrowly functional, like cheers at a football game or an Indian rain-dance. Some is for entertainment, like jazz. Church music will try to accommodate the needs of a worshipping body, while at the same time cultivating an aesthetic dimension. There is music for work, for play, for war, and for a host of other human activities. Each will have ways of meaning that articulate those activities. As in the building, it is not the specifics of colour, wall-length, shape of the roof which determine the meaning. It is all of these things together, in their metaphorical function in relation to the rest of life, which makes for the way in which music means.

4: Spiritual Forces in Music

One aspect of the world of music, whose importance was noted in a preliminary way in the first chapter, is that of its power. Music seems to have certain forces, and many philosophers have pondered them. But not all of these forces are quite the same. There can be emotional impact. There can also be a communication of values and ideals. Some people feel there is even more, and that music can carry with it a certain spiritual power which may lead to moral improvement, or even to moral decadence. How accurate is this idea? How should we approach it?

No-one denies the power of music. As if we needed to have this confirmed, a study by a Stanford University pharmacologist in the December 1985 issue of *Psychology Today* has shown that 'thrills' in response to a musical passage far exceed those from other expected 'thrillers'. Some of the categories are interesting:

Musical passages (96%),
Scene in a movie, play or book (92%),
Great beauty in nature or art (87%),
Physical contact with another person (78%),
Climactic moment in opera (72%),
Sexual activity (70%),
Nostalgic moments (70%).

Of course such surveys are only to be taken half seriously, especially as the criteria for a thrill are 'feeling like a chill, shudder, tingling or tickling, often accompanied by goose bumps, a lump in the throat or weeping'. Still, the fact that a large group of people would consider music's impact greater than that of, say, sex or nostalgia, is significant.

The power of music over the listener has been observed from Plato to Unesco. The Bible writers acknowledge it as well. When the city of Jericho fell, it was to the sounds of the priests' trumpets (Josh. 6.16). David was able to refresh Saul, sending away an evil spirit from him, through playing

79

the lyre (1 Sam. 16.23; 18.10; 19.9). Music is also associated with prophecy in the Old Testament. The 'bands of prophets' who seem to have operated as a school often accompanied their prophetic utterances with music (1 Sam. 10.5−6). It was the duty of the sons of Asaph, Heman and Jeduthun, appointed by David, to 'prophesy with lyres, with harps, and with cymbals' (1 Chron. 25.1). When Elisha predicted the destruction of Moab to the king of Israel, Jehoram, he did so to the accompaniment of a musician: 'And when the minstrel played, the power of the Lord came upon him' (2 Kings 3.14−15).

The simple fact that music is present at the most significant moments in human life is also evidence of this power. What would a wedding be without music? Or a memorial ceremony? Merchants know full well the effects of music on their clients. The omnipresence of piped-in music discussed in the first chapter is testimony to its importance. Naturally this poses certain problems.

The Fear of Music
The Soviet regime has struggled with the place of music for several generations. Cultural intervention was an obvious necessity for Stalin as he directed various purges in the 1930s. The arts in general and music in particular were scrutinized at a high level. The immediate goal was to expunge all traces of bourgeois art from Russia. In music this was done by promoting so-called revolutionary songs, and 'Soviet music for the Soviet variety theatre'. It was also done by efforts on a grand scale by the Commissariat of Public Enlightenment to create a truly indigenous popular culture, free from all outside influences.[1] Thus it was important to suppress jazz, for example, not because of the musical style itself, but because it often connoted cabarets and night clubs and other forms of decadence. Of course, the irony here is that real jazz was a proletarian creation. It was invented by black American slaves! At one point the saxophone was banned from the Soviet Union, though not for very long. An organization called the Association of Proletarian Musicians became a semi-official censorship body. It decided to operate by the classic consumer-based approach of finding out what the people really wanted in music. The catch was that the

word 'really' meant the Association had the right to measure the degree to which public taste had been corrupted by bourgeois propaganda. Applying the circular Marxist argument of 'false consciousness' the Association eventually decided that it alone was capable of determining what the true proletarian market really was. The government accepted this authority more and more, and finally, again by tragic irony, the existing basis for popular initiative in the arts, including popular music, was done away with.[2]

We recognize this pattern as one of fear and manipulation. In the light of Soviet ideology it is an entirely legitimate fear in one way. The power of music being what it is, removing all questionable intrusions which might reflect bourgeois ideology is essential. In another sense, however, this fear is inconsistent. Popular art simply cannot be created from above.

Christians in the West have not entirely escaped this kind of fear. While in principle the Reformation held to a coherent approach to life (*coram deo*, as the classical orthodox reformed theologians would put it), a secondary stream of mysticism challenged the spirit of the Reformation view. As Professor Rookmaaker once put it:

> This mystical stream often depreciated everything outside the 'spiritual', the 'religious' in the more narrow sense. It must have had a stronger influence than we often assume, as only in this way can we understand why psalm-singing, which was originally very lively, cheerful and attractive (Queen Elizabeth once called the Psalms 'Geneva jigs'!) was abandoned for a very slow and almost unmusical way of singing—the sort of thing against which Isaac Watts later protested, and which was only superseded by the vigorous hymn-singing of the Wesleyans.[3]

This 'slow and almost unmusical way of singing' refers to a practice called 'lining-out' which was a way of singing hymns whereby a precentor sings the first line, and the congregation follows by imitation. This practice was probably a necessity among the poorer members of the Dissenter branch of Protestant Christianity. Nevertheless, even in the musical reforms of the Methodists popular songs were forbidden.[4]

John Calvin himself was perhaps partially to blame for this fear of music. Not that he did not enormously appreciate music. Several passages from his writings testify to his aesthetic sense in general and his love of music in particular. In his Commentary on Genesis 4.20 he notes that although music exists for our enjoyment rather than for our need, 'it ought not on that account to be judged of no value; still less should it be condemned'. His most extensive declarations about music are in his *Preface to the Psalter*.[5] Here he extols music as one of the highest of God's gifts: 'Now among the other things proper to recreate man and give him pleasure, music is either the first or the principal, and we must think that it is a gift of God deputed for that purpose.'

It is strange to discover that Calvin only favoured singing the Psalms, and that without harmony, and with no musical accompaniment by instruments. His reasoning is two-fold. First he can find no better songs for prayer, praise, meditation in order to love, fear, honour and glorify God than the Psalms of David. His concern was to be sure that at the highest point of worship God himself put the words into our mouths.[6] Since for Calvin worship centred on edification, he wanted to make sure no errors crept in at this point. But there is a second, more problematic reason. It has to do with the nature of music, as he viewed it. Calvin was concerned, as was Augustine a thousand years before him,[7] about the power of music to move and sway people. Yet, like Augustine, he may have fallen prey to a Platonic view of that power, one that has much in common with the views we argued against in the previous chapter. We read in the same *Preface to the Psalter*:

> But there is still more, for there is hardly anything in the world with more power to turn or bend ('*tourner ou fléchir*') this way and that, the morals of men, as Plato has prudently considered. And in fact we find by experience that it has a secret and almost incredible power to move our hearts in one way or another.[8]

If we follow up this reference to Plato we discover in the *Republic* an elaborate treatment of the subject, where the philosopher is concerned about the 'tempering effects' of music.[9] He is discussing the value of musical training in the Republic. It is 'a more potent instrument than any other, because rhythm and harmony find their way into the inward places of the soul . . .'. Rightly used, it can make a man 'graceful and harmonious', but abused, it renders him 'melted and softened beyond what is good for him'. Plato then uses

82

an image which Calvin takes up in the *Preface*. He likens the body to a funnel into which music can be poured. When there is excess, the man has 'wasted away his spirit and cut out the sinews of his soul'. Calvin transforms the image somewhat. Music becomes the funnel through which good or evil words can be poured. The melody makes the content pierce the heart 'much more strongly', so that should the words be evil they are the more easily poured in, so that 'venom and corruption are distilled to the very depths of the heart by melody'.

The problem is not Calvin's healthy respect for the power of music. It is rather his fear of music as a vehicle for evil. To be sure, one must not divorce music from content. If it is metaphorically powerful it does relate to content, paradigms and even world-views. But not in a neutral way. Calvin does not seem to have thought about musical structure as a crucial aspect of the content. He does say that the melodies should be tempered with the gravity that is fitting in the sight of God, lending grace and dignity to religious actions. Music in the service should not be composed merely for sweetness and delight, but should be becoming of the majesty of worship.[10] Yet he opted for the suppression of instrumental accompaniment because he felt the use of instruments in worship to be no longer necessary. That use is to stir up the souls of the sluggish and dull! He shared this fear of music with the Church Fathers, who were hostile toward the use of instruments in worship. They were not, of course, opposed to music as such, but rather its abuse in the pagan banquets and rituals.[11] However, the effect of these views on Calvin was to encourage his mistrust.

The problem for us is that there is much truth in the fear expressed. Music does have a particular power to move, and it is therefore to be handled with great care by those who make use of it. Nevertheless that is not sufficient reason to put it at a distance. At any rate, rather than focus the same intensity of reforming zeal on music and the arts, many Protestants since Calvin's time have failed to deal biblically and wisely with music, with the result that this 'mystical stream' has been with us constantly. At times the anti-musical fervour of Evangelicals went so far that entire social classes were alienated from the gospel. A quote from Edward Jones on this matter in the Welsh revivals illustrates dramatically:

> The sudden decline of the national Minstrelsy, and Customs of Wales, is in a great degree to be attributed to the fanatick imposters, or illiterate plebeian preachers, who have too often been suffered to over-run the country, misleading the greater part of the common people from their lawful Church; and dissuading them from their innocent amusements, such as Singing, Dancing, and other rural Sports and Games, which heretofore they had been accustomed to delight in, from the earliest times. In the course of my excursions through the Principality, I have met with several Harpers and Songsters, who actually had been prevailed upon by those erratic strollers to relinquish their profession, from the idea that it was sinful.[12]

Certainly this reaction is nourished by more than merely aesthetic considerations, but it is indicative of the fact that often revivalist approaches to spirituality put cultural considerations together with 'the world' in a realm to be suspected of grave dangers, rather than to be redeemed.

Rock and Roll

The most recent candidate for fear is clearly rock music. As we said in the first chapter, rock is a major force today. Although it has strong roots in the Rhythm and Blues music of black Americans, it has developed into a distinct (though much varied) entity. It is most easily recognized by its strong pulsation, usually emphasizing the second and fourth beat of the measure. To many Christians it represents the worldly style *par excellence.* Both the music and the words are frequently cited as cause for alarm.

On the musical level the argument usually involves a strong commitment to the view that music's primary effect is psychophysiological. In the most extreme forms, rock is seen to manipulate human beings through the acoustical means at its disposal. Régimbal, for example, describes the use of subversive signals speaking to the sub-conscious mind through such devices as a regular beat, high-pitched sounds, and the 'backward masking process' whereby occult messages are encoded in the lyrics so that if they are reversed, or played backward by the mind, they can influence the psyche. One example he uses is *Stairway to Heaven*, a popular song in the seventies by the group Led Zeppelin. When played backwards on a special turntable, it seems to repeat the words 'I've got to live for Satan', over and over.[13] This sort of view is occasionally shared by the musicians themselves. The late Jimi Hendrix once said: 'You can hypnotize people with music and when they get at their weakest point, you can preach into their subconscious minds what you want to say'.[14] Plato's shadow lurks again in such views of music. Still it is important not to ignore certain aspects of the darker side of rock.

It is true that the message of rock is not always healthy. Quite the opposite in some cases. Some of the best-selling hits in recent times are carriers of strong statements on rebellion against authority, drug abuse, sexual promiscuity, violence and the occult. The nine million seller by Prince, *Purple Rain*, contains the song *Darling Nikki*, which has the following lyric:

> I knew a girl named Nikki . . . I guess you could say she was a sex fiend. I met her in a hotel lobby, masturbating with a magazine . . . I couldn't resist when I saw little Nikki grind.[15]

One also finds plenty of references to nihilism in rock, often coupled with themes of violence. Despite claims that young people listen only to the beat and the melody, it is unlikely that words such as these have no effect, especially when certain performance practices are coupled with the message, such as spitting blood and burning guitars.

While in this case the fear of music seems legitimate enough, it is important to point out certain weaknesses in the purely alarmist approach espoused by some. One of them is the tendency to group all rock and roll together into one dangerous type. Yet there are many varieties of rock, and many different musicians whose commitments and paradigms vary greatly. The number of rock bands actually committed to promoting easy sex, violence and the occult is smaller than some of rock's critics would have us think. Or, at least it could be said that rock lyrics do not speak any more explicitly and frequently on these topics than other art forms and the media in general. This does not make it right, of course, but nor does it single out rock or music as exceptional vehicles of decadent values.

85

The fundamental question is whether the music itself can manipulate people into accepting a message they otherwise would not be disposed to accept. To pose the question this way is to raise several issues at once. How extensive is music's power? What is it able to move in us? How important is the human will in order to be moved? Is it proper to speak of manipulation at all?

In the previous chapter we argued against over-emphasizing the psycho-acoustical signification (way of meaning) in music. Quite often those who tend to reject rock because of its power to corrupt argue on this ground. The regular pulse of the beat, played on loud drums, is meant to 'get into the bloodstream' and mesmerize the listener. Anyone who has been to a rock concert can testify to the apparent truth of this claim. Certain performers are able to induce mass hysteria in their audiences.

Music and Manipulation

There are two ways to approach the matter in order to test for a measurable psycho-acoustical effect. There is a growing body of behavioural studies on the physical and psychological effects of music on the listener. Unfortunately the data are not at all clear. A number of specialists have tentatively concluded that there is some correlation between certain types of music and modified physiological activities such as breathing, cardio-vascular patterns and galvanic skin response. Even with these there often come in extra-physical factors, such as previous experience in the music world, or even tiredness and emotional predisposition.[16] From this vague beginning to moral manipulation there are light years of distance.

A second, more helpful way to measure the effect of music is the comparative method. A number of studies have been done on the relation of music to certain types of behaviour across the world. The most thorough to date is Gilbert Rouget's *La musique et la transe*.[17] This ethnomusicologist compared hundreds of cases in widely different cultures where a state of trance is induced, in order to find out what role music plays. His definition of trance is quite broad, although it is not the same thing for him as ecstasy. The trance is a change of state whereby a person becomes something else, as it were, or is invaded by something else. It most often involves movement, noise, some sort of sensory stimulation, amnesia and hysteria. It is a public occurrence. Ecstasy, on the other hand, is an individual happening, done in silence, without crisis, often as a result of deprivation of some kind. In ecstasy there can be hallucination, whereas this is not the case of trance.[18] Rouget's study is primarily on trance, which is particularly interesting for us, since according to his broad definition the folly and hysteria at a rock concert would qualify as being a similar experience to the trance-like state in other cultures. Music is often (though not universally) present as an important factor in bringing on the state of trance. But its actual power to induce is not simple to grasp. Almost everyone from the various societies considered acknowledges the crucial importance of music in the achievement of the state of trance (or in coming back from it), but there is no consistent explanation of the dynamics of that relation.

Rouget compares many different groups in order to establish norms. What kind of sound is required? Vocal? instrumental? what instruments? Some societies insist on the presence of musical instruments. But the state of trance can be induced with only *a capella* singing. This is the case in Tunisia, where singing the *dhikr* is enough to lead into trance. It is also the case in Bali.[19] In many cases where instruments do play a role it is impossible to determine a consistent pattern. Occurrences of every possible variant can be found: singing alternating with instruments, singing with instruments, instruments alone. What types of instruments are used? The answer is every type. No one class of instruments predominates.

The presence of drums should be scrutinized in a particular way since many people attribute special powers to them. In rock music the drum is seen to have an important part in conferring an emotional impact on the listener. Rodney Needham maintains that percussion in general has great powers. In his study of Haitian Voodoo he tries to demonstrate the effects of drumming on heart-beat, blood-pressure and muscle-tone, which lead to certain psychic disorders.[20] Experiments have been done to try and prove the detrimental effects of certain kinds of drumming (both in terms of pitch-frequency and pulse rate) on convulsive behaviour.[21] Unfortunately both the observations and the experiments have been sharply contested. If one takes the rhythms of the types of drumming which are supposed to induce convulsions as universally valid, then one ought to find people in a state of convulsion all over the world, since these rhythms are found in a good many places. But we don't.[22] In the present state of the research there are no valid theories, backed up by sound observation, which allow us to say drums can lead to modified behaviour on neurophysiological grounds.

The same problem exists if one attempts to isolate a certain type of music that goes with the trance. Sometimes it is simple and repetitive. At others it is rather involved. One also finds slow, deliberate chanting, as in the case of Thai Buddhist ceremonial music. On other occasions it is fast and frenetic. There is simply no universal pattern.

What does this leave us with? If psycho-acoustical factors cannot explain the 'strange mechanism' of music's power,[23] what can? Rouget's conclusion is that we are dealing with music's ability to put across a message because it is a sign. This is similar to the idea of metaphor we developed in the previous chapter. The ability of the sign to lead to altered states of consciousness is not in music's physical qualities. It is not the *musical substance* which induces the trance. It is because music is in motion. It reaches our beings because it signifies a way of experiencing space and time. This is why certain melodies bring on a certain feeling. This is why the crowds go into excited frenzy when only the first few notes of a rock star's guitar are played. This is also why music is an *appropriate* accompaniment to the trance ceremonies.[24] Music can help support and intensify an emotional state because of the *way it means in the trance situation.* Often certain divinities are 'known' to prefer certain melodies, and so the people naturally become sensitive to their use. Because music can 'speak' a certain language, it is often *the* appropriate way to indicate a trance.

It is also because music, being what it is, does reach into the depths of human experience. Singing requires involvement at the level of our very breathing. Considering that the human being is defined biblically in terms of the *nefesh*, the animation or breath of life, we should not be surprised that it has such an impact. Even if this impact is not in terms of measurable psycho-acoustical factors, the metaphorical values communicated are carried through sounds ordered in time, and therefore music is a medium whose power is great. This is undoubtedly why so many philosophers and thinkers have observed the unique ability of this art to influence our behaviour. Rouget, far from denying this power, shows that the ability for music to accompany trance-inducement is in a way greater because of its sign value than if it only worked physiologically. Contrary to what many people think, trance music is not simply repetitive and accumulative. It may be quite varied and rich with symbolism of all sorts, making it able to 'modify our being-in-the-world'.[25]

What this all means for our reactions to rock music is not that there aren't aspects of it which are legitimately to be feared. But it means we do not have to fear a conspiracy of manipulation through acoustical devices.[26] What we should look for instead is the true message of rock, as it speaks musically. This means a look at the social factors involved in listening to rock. Why are so many people drawn to it? Why is it one of the major musical forces today? What is it signalling to us? The signal can only be understood in terms of the larger social and musical context in which we find ourselves. To understand rock we must look at it in terms of social architecture in the aspect of sound. It is a covenant response. What kind of response to the covenant do we have? In many cases it would seem to be rebellious. Yet in others it is healthy protest. Most often it is a mixture of the two. Furthermore, when evil is present, it may not be in an overtly aggressive appeal to immorality. The recent trends toward conservatism in some singers may be no less alarming than invitations to decadence. Madonna is a sex-symbol, but her audience is primarily wealthy, materialistic youth. She has been called the Queen of the Yuppies. Financial security may edge out sex:

> Only boys that save their pennies
> Make my rainy day . . .
> We're living in a material world
> And I'm a material girl.[27]

The opposite can be said as well. Some of rock's apparent

invitations to loose living are only honest commentaries on life as it is. In the best tradition of the blues (from which, indirectly or directly, much rock is derived) a good deal of this music is observing 'life under the sun', in very much the same way as the Book of Ecclesiastes in the Bible. It is very important not to lump everything together in a Manichean way, where all becomes black or white, light or darkness.

Power and Freedom

How does this square with the biblical references to power alluded to earlier? Does not the destruction of Jericho by trumpet blasts and the calming of Saul's spirit by David's lyre look very much like the kind of spiritual force so often attributed to psycho-acoustical factors? Let us look very carefully at the passage about David's music-therapy for Saul. The essential text is 1 Samuel 16.14 — 23. The setting for David's service to Saul is that God had rejected Saul. Saul had committed two crimes which earned him removal from office. First, he sacrificed a burnt-offering in order to entreat God's favour against the Philistines, when he had no right to do so (1 Sam. 13.8 — 15). Second, he refused to carry out the Lord's order to act as an instrument of judgement against the Amalekites by destroying them all (15.8 — 16). These two acts amounted to treason, and so God rejected Saul as king over Israel (16.1). God's Spirit thus departed from him, and an 'evil spirit from the Lord' came to torment him. The Holy Spirit was given to Israel's leaders, symbolized by anointing. This enabled them to lead with wisdom and strength (10.10; 11.6; see Num. 11.25, 29; Judg. 14.6). When Saul turned his heart from the Lord, Samuel anointed David in his place: 'and the Spirit of the Lord came mightily upon David from that day forward' (16.13). It might come as a surprise to learn that God would actually send an evil spirit to trouble someone. But this is consistent with biblical parallels about the way God judges unfaithfulness. He is the Lord even of those demonic powers which are fallen, as the opening of the Book of Job reminds us (Job 1.6 — 12; see Zech. 3.1 — 2). In one episode the Lord actually allows a 'lying spirit' to delude the prophets of Israel so that Ahab should be judged (1 Kings 22.19 — 23). Of course it would be unthinkable for God to have created the evil spirit. It had to rebel of its own will to become evil. But once it had rebelled, God could use it for judgement. Notice that the evil spirit does not force men into wrong-doing. It only adds to the intensity of judgement for it.

The next thing to notice is that David was discovered by Saul's servants because of his reputation. He was not only 'skilful in playing' but 'a man of valour, a man of war, prudent in speech, and a man of good presence' (1 Sam. 16.18). He was clearly not brought in as a kind of specialist in exorcism, or even music therapy. In fact the mention of 'prudent in speech' is perhaps indicative of a prophetic office. The word 'prudent' is actually the same Hebrew word which is translated 'skilful' in describing David's ability on the lyre. In other words, he was a minstrel who no doubt sang words, the word of God itself, with his playing. It is true that the text does not mention specifically that David sang. But the connection is often made in other places between the word and musical accompaniment (2 Kings 3.14−15; 1 Chron. 25.1−2; Col. 3.16). The Book of Psalms is replete with examples of this connection. Thus David's role was not only to help out by playing an instrument; he had a broader ministry to Saul. He even became his armour-bearer. He undoubtedly spoke the word of God to him, and may well have sung it, to relieve him from his torments.

Still, the three texts which mention this therapy specifically single out David's playing 'with his hand' (1 Sam. 16.23; 18.10; 19.10). The music does have an important role. What is it? He had to play *well* (16.17). And it is mentioned that he played every day (18.10). This means that the music was not some kind of magic, used as a kind of drug. In fact the Bible has a very strong teaching against the practice of magic, and there is no trace of a magical view of the arts in the affirmations that are made in Scripture. I think that besides its role as accompaniment to the word of God, the music of David helped to create a new architecture for Saul. It helped, because of its powerful metaphorical value, to re-insert Saul into reality, at least temporarily. It did not succeed each time. Twice Saul threw a spear at him, jealous as he was of the favour David had found in the eyes of the people (18.11; 19.9). This is another proof that we are not dealing with magic.[28]

The priests' horns in the story of the conquest of Jericho

are even more clearly metaphorical. They are signs, even signals (Joshua 6.4, 8−9, 16). Again the music is combined with the human voice. And the trumpets were probably the 'jubilee trumpets' which God commanded the people to use for special occasions in order to announce his theophanic presence (see Lev. 25.9−10). In any case, the trumpet was often used by the priests to signify a special act of God, but never in a magical sense. And there is no indication in the text of Joshua that the walls of the city fell because of destructive vibrations (Josh. 6.20). Rather, the Book of Hebrews, commenting on this event, tells us it was 'by faith' that the walls fell (Heb. 11.30). Faith means that the people *expected* God to give the victory, just as in the case of crossing the Red Sea (Heb. 11.29).

It is very important to underscore this. The role of faith shows us the place of human freedom in relation to the power unleashed. In certain cases the power of music can be resisted, even when it comes from God. Jesus himself alludes to this in a most significant statement which deals with music, at least indirectly:

'But to what shall I compare this generation? It is like children sitting in the market places and calling to their playmates,
   "We piped to you, and you did not dance;
   we wailed and you did not mourn."' (Matt. 11.16−17)

The power of music therefore can be resisted. Human beings are free agents, even to the point where they can reject the truth itself.[29] But it can also work the other way. They can resist the power of music which is meant to be seductive. Just as the Lord can say to unfaithful Israel, 'Take away from me the noise of your songs; to the melody of your harps I will not listen' (Amos 5.23), so we may freely reject music which articulates evil.

This is why regimes which base their musical censorship on the psycho-acoustical view of music must fail. They will inevitably oversimplify the problems, singling out songs and styles which supposedly induce 'nervous spasms' and promote 'negative spiritual life', and passing over songs which really might convey an ideology which is dangerous to the state. Music is indeed a powerful way to convey a message. In the Epistle to the Ephesians its use is coupled with the filling of

92

the Spirit (5.18—19). But like the Spirit's action, although it is invisible it is not manipulative. Music is also coupled with teaching the word of Christ (Col. 3.16). Music involves rational structures despite its aesthetic orientation, or rather because of it (if properly understood). It is for us to discern them, in the light of biblical norms for truth.

Where Is the Evil?
The principles elaborated above are easier to set forth than their application. Yet it is important not to leave the matter of spiritual forces hanging in the air. Let us try to identify a few cases of the negative power in this section. We shall want to spend more time on the constructive side in our last chapter.

Of course, evil is not a 'thing'. It cannot be identified with matter, as the Manicheans thought. Evil is difficult to define . . . as it should be. Its essence is to have no essence. It is only really definable in opposition to the good. Evil is *contra boni*. Not that it is unreal. It is painfully real, as the fallen world we live in testifies.[30] It is certainly no illusion. Rebellion is real. Although evil is primarily a moral consideration, there are effects in the world. There is a state of evil: 'the whole world is in the power of the evil one' (1 John 5.19). But the characteristics of evil are lust, and pride (1 John 2.16).

The identification of evil can never be in the particular notes and rhythms of the music as isolated entities, therefore. It must be in the compositional and structural features. There are many ways in which this can be manifest. And of course nothing made by human beings, not even an abstract art-form like music, is ever totally evil (or totally good). Human beings remain in the image of God despite the fall, and God keeps them from becoming absolutely corrupt. There will be tendencies one way or another, but never total 'success' in their articulation.

One of the strong tendencies in the art music of the twentieth century can be singled out for scrutiny. It is what I would call egalitarianism. Rooted in the spirit of revolution in the nineteenth century, egalitarianism, along with two other ideals in the well-known slogan, liberty and fraternity, is the desire to break down distinctions and to equalize from above. I am not referring to the legitimate pursuit of equal justice or equal opportunity before the law, but to the systematic

93

abolition of all hierarchy in an attempt to establish a utopian society based on human reason rather than divine revelation. Many experiments in such utopias have been tried, from Saint Simon's community to the Paris Commune, to Bolshevism. While art is not a seismometer, recording each tremor on earth, it does reflect the major ideologies of an era.

Revolutionary ideals are not restricted to overt political conflict. Sometimes the most revolutionary initatives are in cultural areas seemingly far removed from current events. And sometimes they occur during periods of relative calm. Such a time was the late nineteenth century and the early twentieth. The 'empire' period enveloped Europe in a blanket of apparent security. Much of the music of that time was either lifeless or decadent. But a few composers were busily setting the tone for the rest of the modern age. Claude Achille Debussy (1867 — 1918) has only recently been recognized as a leader of the spirit of egalitarian music. Some have even called him the father of modern music. He expressed his antipathy to established conventions early in his career. Although he did his formal training at the Paris Conservatory, and won the coveted Prix de Rome in composition, he rejected the classical orientation he received there. After winning the Prix he announced, 'Je sentis que je n'étais plus libre.'[31] This youthful iconoclasm became a mature aesthetic. He longed to discover new forms to express his need to become free from 'a world that is too correct'.

One of the best illustrations of what he did discover is *La Mer*, a three-part symphonic sketch written in 1905. As the title suggests, it was a musical analogy to the movement of the sea. And it is characteristic of a large body of water that although it moves and undulates, it never goes, as it were, from A to Z. There is no linear progression, but only moments and eternal flow. One of the musical devices he used is the well-known whole-tone scale. In it each note is one step apart, unlike the traditional diatonic scale in which there is an uneven distribution of intervals. It is a rather literal type of musical egalitarianism, since each note is equidistant. It evokes a feeling of ambiguity, mystery and suspense. The whole-tone scale is frequently used in movie music at the appropriate scene. Chords built with notes from this scale are functionally 'unstable' and can be resolved in different ways.

94

Debussy often does not resolve them at all.

What is most egalitarian, however, is not this fundamental note selection, with its special colour, but the formal design of the piece. It is a spun-out series of 'moments' or 'happenings'. No theme is ever developed beyond a few bars (measures). There are no principal or subordinate melodies. The ephemeral movement of waves and wind are articulated in terms of musical cell units in succession. Each one is compact, complete in itself. Timbre is more important than architecture. After listening to the piece we feel we have experienced something intangible. We have been looking at a mobile turning every which way, but always on itself. The whole seems to be more important than the fleeting parts. Of course the sounds are fascinating and lovely at the sensuous level. But the paradigm is one of relativity rather than development.

Do we have a parallel between this kind of musical egalitarianism and an aesthetic principle in contemporary art? Paul Gauguin attempted to translate nature, and especially feelings about nature, into colours. His techniques at times made men and women, trees, mountains all merge into mere contrasts of colour and line. The unity seems to consume all differences.[32] In the search for universals the art of many of the best painters became abstract, reaching for pure form.

Anton von Webern, as we saw, brought the egalitarian ideal much further. In his lectures, *The Path to the New Music*, given in 1932 and 1933,[33] he discussed the history of music. He saw it as a 'quest for comprehensibility and unity'. Each period is a new 'conquest', whereby an old style is exhausted and replaced by a new one which is more 'unified'. In the modern period major and minor modes disappear, and are replaced by the chromatic scale, wherein notes have no special functional value in relation to a key centre.[34] Composers must now discover a system to *prevent* any one note from being too much emphasized. The traditional round does this somewhat, but it is not egalitarian enough. Webern discovered a new 'law'. He called it 'the round of twelve notes'. He tried different methods of equalizing the notes of the chromatic scale. There are only twelve different ones in traditional western music.

One of the first pieces which uses this principle in a consistent way is *Opus 13, No. 1*. It is a setting of a poem by the expressionist poet K. Kraus. Here are three bars (measures) from the piece.

Notice the intricate way in which the notes relate to one another. The intervals between them run in series of three. There is a pivot point which defines the relationship of the notes before and after, or over and under. Thus, a series of mirror effects seem to translate the words (*Spiegel* in German is a mirror) into note relationships.

Webern was a pantheist. His music was written because of an inner compulsion toward total unity: 'The further one presses forward, the greater becomes the identity of everything, and finally we have the impression of being faced by a work not of man but of nature.'[35] His life as he describes it was a search for the hidden *Word* behind all things. He believed that the way to find it was to create music which was more and more unified. Listening to it, we discover God. This is in fact a kind of idolatry. Music becomes a way of salvation.[36] It is a small step from Webern's view to those of more recent composers like Boulez and Stockhausen who have gone very far in order to abolish distinctions. They have serialized all parameters. Stockhausen bases his work on what he calls the 'principle of mediation'. According to him, all parts of reality are connected. There is no black or white, only grey. Flowers, sand, sky, brains, machines, all things are in continuity. Electronic music is superbly qualified to render this principle into sound, since it is important to go beyond the limits of traditional western instruments. Only synthesizers can produce the nuances of sounds that correspond to the shades of grey in his philosophy. Human beings are absorbed into the whole as they listen. They merge into the all.

I do not want to give the reader the impression that there is not much to draw from in the music of many serialist composers. Neither artists nor anyone else can successfully build a world which totally contradicts the structures of reality, the structures of God's created world, governed by his covenant presence. And so there are many beauties to be found in some of this strange musical texture. This raises the important question of how to use these positive features without falling into the dogmatism of orthodox serialism. We will deal with that in the following chapter. Furthermore, it must be stressed that serialism is only one trend among many in the twentieth century. While its claims are particularly insistent, this hardly justifies the occasional pretention to exclusivity that one hears. The whole notion of an 'avant-garde' movement is difficult to accept, in fact. While innovations have always been met with a mixed reception in the past, we seem to have a much larger gap between tradition and innovation in the twentieth century than ever before. The music of this pantheistic current we are discussing has broken with tradition at the most fundamental level. And some of it has gone to great extremes to demonstrate that break.

More recently composers have melted down all of reality, so that even people become motifs for composition. Some of them like to wire-up the human body, attaching terminals to the head and to various organs in order to turn brainwaves and other pulsations into sounds. Taken further, the whole environment can become a sound source. In Paul Oliveros's *Bonn Fire* an entire city becomes the source for music. This

radical pantheism, which melts all things down in the hopes
of finding God, is idolatry. It is evil in music. It is a rebellion
against the structured order of the created universe.

This happens when people want to ignore the principles
elucidated previously. Music is not seen to be human covenant
response in the aspect of ordered sound. Rather it becomes a
means of salvation. André Malraux believed that in our
century art has replaced the Christian belief in God, because
we can no longer accept theological language, but we do
accept aesthetic language.[37] I think this is true. And when it
happens, a far greater burden is placed on art than it is meant
to have. Not only does it speak (metaphorically) of non-
Christian principles, but it speaks too much altogether. We
could illustrate this as in the diagram below.

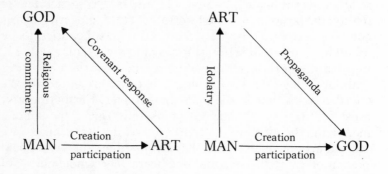

The biblical pattern is for human beings to worship God, and
to have their ultimate commitment to him. This means that
creating art-forms is a secondary activity which nonetheless
reflects our primary commitment. Our art is offered up to
God in covenant response. On the other side artistic creation
becomes a substitute for the primary commitment to God.
Art must save, and therefore it bears the heavy burden of
replacing God. As such it becomes propaganda and must
express 'revelatory' truths about God and other parts of
reality. Man participates in divinity because he trusts in art.

It must not be thought that only art music in its most élite
expression can be identified as idolatrous. If this were true
relatively few people would be affected.[38] The recent rock
film *Purple Rain* conveyed the same view, but in the medium

of popular music and rock stars. The hero, Prince, is a confused, angry person whose profession is music-making. His family life is abysmal, and he is so proud that he can barely get along with his fellow performers. In the end, though, he is saved . . . through music. Rock saves! Of course, we are not told this in so many words, but the film puts across the idea by showing reconciliations between Prince and the other musicians in the act of performing. Playing rock leads you to a better world. A good number of contemporary video-clips give the same impression. Some of them are frankly pagan, with cut-up scenes and absurd sequences to confuse our minds and prepare them to meet the irrational. All kinds of devices like open windows, artificial fog, musicians placed on stage like priests for a ritual, are used to produce the effect. These are the real spiritual forces in music. They are far more powerful than just the use of acoustical devices. They are metaphors and allusions to evil in the medium of ordered sound, a medium which articulates meaning at a deep level.

What is the reason for this rebellion? Where does the drive come from? The psalmist asks the same question:

> Why do the nations conspire,
>   and the peoples plot in vain?
> The kings of the earth set themselves,
>   and the rulers take counsel together,
>   against the Lord and his anointed, saying,
> 'Let us burst their bonds asunder,
>   and cast their cords from us.' (Ps. 2.1 – 3)

But the question does not receive an answer. In fact nowhere in the Bible is there an explanation for evil. Any explanation would justify it, and even excuse it. Evil remains a mystery. Why do human beings rise up against the ultimate origin of the universe? While we are responsible, there is no reason. But there is a solution to evil, even if there is no explanation. Our psalm goes on, and concludes:

> Now therefore, O kings, be wise;
>   be warned, O rulers of the earth.
> Serve the Lord with fear,
>   with trembling kiss his feet,

    lest he be angry, and you perish in the way;
        for his wrath is quickly kindled.
    Blessed are all who take refuge in him. (vv. 10—11)

If there are spiritual forces in music which stem from idolatry,
there are also forces for the good, which stem from the wise
service of the Lord. Let us look into some of those in the
next chapter.

5: Making Melody to the Lord

It is always easier to identify negative factors than to go on to say how something should be done positively. Staying with the negative is not a scriptural approach. The full context for the above title is this: .

> Therefore do not be foolish, but understand what the will of the Lord is. And do not get drunk with wine, for that is debauchery; but be filled with the Spirit, addressing one another in psalms and hymns and spiritual songs, singing and making melody to the Lord with all your heart, always and for everything giving thanks in the name of our Lord Jesus Christ to God the Father. (Eph. 5.17—20)

It is an amazing passage on several accounts. First, the balance struck between what I have called the negative and the positive. Being foolish is rejected in favour of understanding the will of the Lord. Drunkenness is rejected in favour of being filled with the Spirit. And music comes in here. In contrast to wine, which can lead to prodigality (*asōtia*), the Spirit of God edifies and builds up. The Spirit's presence is not only manifest but invoked by community singing! This is partly because of his close witness to the Word of God, as the parallel passage in Colossians 3.16 attests. And it is partly, I believe, because of the unique ability music has to 'speak' to the heart.

Indeed, only a heart which is renewed by the Holy Spirit can begin to show any kind of love and gratitude at all, although it will never be perfect in this life (see Titus 3.1—7). In other words the 'new song', which we have already talked about, emanates from a 'new heart'. When we believe, we can be considered alive in a new sense, alive from the heart: '. . . you are a letter from Christ delivered by us, written not with ink but with the Spirit of the living God, not on tablets of stone but on tablets of human hearts' (2 Cor. 3.3).

Now, this is all very well and good, but what does it actually tell us about the way we should sing and make

101

melody? Is it enough just to have renewed hearts, and thus be 'qualified' for worship? Or are there particular rules and principles which can be applied? In the Romantic view what was needed was genius. From this all else flowed, including musical creativity. But judging from the very different kinds of musical styles which claim to be Christian, it would be difficult to apply this approach to music-making for the Lord. In fact we want to know not only what styles to adopt, but how to make good music. It is hard enough to be correct; it is even harder to be beautiful. As Madeleine L'Engle once put it:

> *Christian* art? Art is art; painting is painting; music is music; a story is a story. If it's bad art, it's bad religion, no matter how pious the subject. If it's good art — and there the questions start coming, questions which it would be simpler to evade.[1]

Called to Make Music

Going back to a few of the principles developed in chapter 2, it is important to remember that music is for everyone in one sense, but in another, it is a vocation addressed to those who have been specially endowed with musical ability. We have argued that this vocation is a cultural one, although it inevitably carries a religious meaning. And we have further argued that this kind of cultural activity continues to have an important place even after the Fall into sin. This fact is not always appreciated in the modern Church. In the apocalyptic times in which we live it is understandable that many Christians want to place all their eggs in the basket of evangelism. Opportunity appears to be running out, and any activity which ties us down to this world is seen as either a waste or at least very secondary. Jesus himself tells us 'Do not labour for the food which perishes, but for the food which endures to eternal life' (John 6.27). And yet it is a great mistake to underscore the urgency of evangelism in such a way as to minimize cultural activity.

When our Lord gave the 'Great Commission' to the Church he never intended to set up a rivalry between evangelism and cultural activity. A careful reading of his words proves the contrary.

> And Jesus came and said to them, 'All authority in heaven and on earth has been given to me. Go therefore and make disciples of all

nations, baptizing them in the name of the Father and of the Son and of the Holy Spirit, teaching them to observe all that I have commanded you; and lo, I am with you always, to the close of the age.' (Matt. 28.18 – 20)

First of all a common error must be corrected. Many people tend to isolate the first words, 'Go therefore' from the rest. Interestingly enough, in the Greek original there are four verbs in that sentence, but only one of them is in the imperative. The other three are participles. The main, imperative verb is not 'go' but 'make disciples'. The other three, 'go', 'baptize', and 'teach' are participles, which means they accompany the principal verb, but have less weight. They are in fact *the way* to make disciples: by going, baptizing and teaching. The point is that 'going' is only one aspect of the larger concept, which is to make disciples. Many Christians tend to put it the other way round, with a kind of psychological pressure to place missionary activity above the broader activity of training people to follow Jesus.

Discipleship means learning the discipline of the master. This includes many types of activities and attitudes. It is much broader than the 'go therefore' of missions. The fact that Jesus made discipleship the great priority for his Church is significant. This is reinforced by the presence of the last verb, to 'teach'. Our Lord wants the Church to teach people to observe *all* that he has commanded, not just 'how to evangelize'. The teachings of Jesus apply to every sphere of life, including the arts and music. It is therefore wrong to erect the pyramid view of Christian calling, with missionaries and pastors on top, and other professions next, and (usually) politics on the bottom. There is no hierarchy of callings in the body of Christ.

Looking at the full passage we see something else that is crucial. There is a preamble and a postscript which are very much part of the text. When Jesus says 'all authority in heaven and on earth has been given to me', he is not simply giving encouraging words to missionaries who work under difficult conditions. He is speaking of the new age inaugurated by God the Father in response to the active obedience of his Son. As he tells in the Revelation, John, while sojourning on the Isle of Patmos, witnesses a dramatic re-enactment of the coming into power of Jesus the Messiah. He sees the Lion of the tribe of Judah come into possession of the scroll of history with its seven seals, because of his worthiness (Rev. 5.1 – 14; see Daniel 7.13 – 14). In the Great Commission the Church is being told that this new age has come, and that the rule of Christ has begun. To be sure we are not yet in the resurrection state of the final consummation. 'Would that you did reign,' says Paul to the Corinthians (1 Cor. 4.8). We certainly do not *see* everything in subjection to Christ (Heb. 2.8). Yet he does reign, so that nothing is outside of his control (Heb. 2.9). The day is at hand (Rev. 13.12), and we can expect 'times of refreshing . . . from the presence of the Lord' (Acts 3.19).

Thus, our calling is in the light of this christological authority in a new age. Making disciples will only be possible because of this heavenly power. Becoming a Christian in medicine, in politics, in construction or in the arts is quite vain unless Christ reigns. Discipleship in one of those spheres may involve personal contact ('go therefore'), it may mean initiation into the Christian community ('baptizing them'), and it may mean systematic and regular instruction in the principles of revealed truth ('teaching them'), but it must fundamentally mean joyful submission to the King of Kings, to whom all authority has been given.

Then there is the postscript. Jesus is with us to the close of the age. Not only does he have power over all things, but he is present with his people in covenant fellowship. Not only will he regularly strengthen us so that we may persevere (Heb. 12.3), but he attends our every activity through the presence of the Spirit. This is far broader than evangelism. It means we receive 'the spirit of wisdom and of revelation in the knowledge of him, having the eyes of your hearts enlightened, that you may know what is the hope to which he has called you, what are the riches of his glorious inheritance in the saints, and what is the immeasurable greatness of his power in us who believe' (Eph. 1.18 – 19). Our calling to particular tasks, such as music-making, has its fullest meaning in this larger context of the presence of the Lord. His dwelling with his people means that they become stewards of the good gifts he bestows on them (see Eph. 4.7 – 12, and 1 Pet. 4.10 – 11). The purpose of this stewardship is indeed to build up the Church. But it is also to live in the fullness of Christ's presence, and to live in the world while not being of the world (John 17.14).

We can begin to appreciate how much the Great Commission is set in the context of all of biblical teaching, and especially of the Cultural Mandate of Genesis 1.28. Because behind the missionary mandate lies the universal mandate to the human race: 'Be fruitful and multiply, and fill the earth and subdue it' (Gen. 1.28). Thus the original mandate takes on a dimension unimagined by its first subjects. Although the terms are modified in accordance with the needs of a postlapsarian age, the basic content is the same from the first to the second mandates. Multiplication is now heightened in the New Covenant. We still must procreate after the Fall (Jer. 30.19; 33.22; Ezek. 36.10−11, 37; 37.26). But we spread the truth of the gospel by the one who fills all things with the Spirit (Eph. 1.22−3; 4.10−13). Thus in the new age there is a kind of spiritual procreation as well as a physical one. Dominion is also heightened in the New Covenant. We still are lords over the earth with all things under our feet (Ps. 8.6). But 'all things' includes death, Satan, and every obstacle to the truth (Heb. 2.9; Rom. 16.20; 2 Cor. 10.4). So both multiplication and dominion are heightened, and fulfilled in Christ. There is therefore no conflict between the so-called natural gifts and the spiritual gifts. Both are gifts of the Spirit. Commenting on the presence of culture in Genesis 4, Calvin said:

> The experience of all ages teaches us how widely the rays of divine light have shone on unbelieving nations, for the benefit of the present life; and we see, at the present time, that the excellent gifts of the Spirit are diffused through the whole human race; moreover, the liberal arts and sciences have descended to us from the heathen.[2]

Taken in its full context, then, the Great Commission cannot be made to build an artificial wall between evangelism and cultural activity. There is no ultimate tension between the Church as a missionary body and the Church as promoter of culture. Of course it would be lopsided to emphasize culture at the expense of evangelism. This is the opposite danger to the one many Evangelical churches have fallen into today. It is just as unbiblical to forget the cutting evangelistic edge in our activities as to forget the cultural dimension. Some Christians seem willing to pursue their cultural involvements without being aware that 'the form of this world is passing away'. Culture must not become an end in itself. A Christian vocation in the arts is Christian not only because the called are moral and honest people in their work, but because they know they are living in the end times, and that 'the end of all things is at hand' (1 Pet. 4.7).

Much of the false tension can be reduced when we realize one more thing about the Great Commission. It is addressed neither to an individual, nor even to a group of individuals, but to the Church, represented by the believing disciples. We all have a particular place and calling within that body, but no single person can exercise all the gifts. When Jesus commands the Church to baptize and to teach he does not mean for every member to engage in performing the baptism ceremony, nor does he mean for everyone to take on the teaching ministry. The Church must assign these tasks to those individuals who are qualified, according to the gifts they have received. It is the same in regard to evangelism and artistic calling. Not all individuals are called to be evangelists. Nor are they all to be experts in every field. But when the gifts function properly, being given to the entire community, there is room for individual vocations which may specialize in one area or another.

Is there a specific call to make music? Of this there can be no doubt. Of course the New Testament lists of church gifts do not mention music-making as one of the gifts. There are two reasons for the omission. For one thing, the lists are not exhaustive. Not only do the various lists differ, but some of them refer to categories rather than to individual 'charismata'. For another, these are church gifts, which are enumerated in the Epistles for the purpose of running the affairs of the visible community of believers. The gifts mentioned were those which needed to be emphasized in relation to problems in the early Church, but they cannot be considered to cover all the problems of living in the world. Marriage is a gift! (see 1 Cor. 7.7).

The visible Church is certainly a true embodiment of the Kingdom of God. The forces of the Kingdom, the life of the Kingdom are manifest in the earthly organisms of the Church.

But this does not mean that the Church is the only outward expression of these forces and this life. God's kingship is meant to rule over the whole of human life in every form of its expression. There are various spheres which must not be confused, but which must all come under the rule of God's sovereignty. The family, the state, the place of work, each of these must come under the supremacy of God's truth. The New Testament does not often make explicit reference to these things, yet it is clear that the general principles of the Kingdom are far broader ones than that which is necessary to church life as such. Besides, it is abundantly clear in the New Testament that our Lord never intended to reach the result of the coming of his Kingdom by subjecting all these spheres to the visible Church. Neither are Church and state to be confused (Matt. 22.21; John 18.36; 19.11; Rom. 13.1; 1 Cor. 6.1−6), nor are other spheres to blend into the Church (1 Tim. 3.4).

To insist on the separate function of each sphere is not to relegate the Church to a secondary position. While every province of life must be brought under the loving control of God, this cannot take place unless the Spirit of God is introduced into the world through the Word. Thus the Church, which is called the 'pillar and bulwark of the truth' (1 Tim. 3.15), has the crucial role of dispensing the means of grace to a lost world. So there is a delicate relationship between the Church and the other spheres of life which manifest the regenerate life of the Kingdom. Geerhardus Vos puts it this way:

> It is entirely in accordance with the spirit of Jesus's teaching to subsume these [branches into which the organic life of humanity divides itself] under the kingdom of God and to co-ordinate them with the visible Church as true manifestations of this kingdom, in so far as the divine sovereignty and glory have become in them the controlling principle. But it must always be remembered, that the latter can only happen, when all these, no less than the visible Church, stand in living contact with the forces of regeneration supernaturally introduced into the world by the Spirit of God. While it is proper to separate between the visible Church and such things as the Christian state, Christian art, Christian science, etc., these things, if they truly belong to the Kingdom of God, grow up out of the regenerated life of the invisible Church.[3]

107

The call to make music is then a call in this larger context. It is not restricted to being a 'church musician', although that is a perfectly legitimate vocation. Music-making becomes a calling within the Kingdom of God, in the age of the rule of Christ. It is a response to the divine gift. This gift is kindled and nurtured in relation to the Church, but it is exercised in the world, in the various places appropriate to making music. Where are these? To that matter we must now turn.

Back to the World of Music
It is important to remember that human capacities, which we may call gifts, do not exist as ends in themselves. They are meant to be exercised in the world. The first men were told to till and keep a garden. They were presumably to make it into a place which was at the same time a lovely habitation and a glory to God. The musician is also called to 'till and keep' his environment. As ruler over God's world, he must find his place in the world of music and attend to its becoming a lovely environment for his dwelling and a glory to God. A little further below we will look into some suggestions for the music itself. But first it seems proper to deal with the terrain, with the place of service. This is not only a biblical priority but frequently the practical one musicians face.

Rather than attempting to be exhaustive, let us examine a few possible places for the musician seeking to bring God's Kingdom to earth in the world. First we might think of the home. At first glance it might appear that our homes are full of music-making. What living-room is not equipped with high-fidelity apparatus ready to play background music? What young person does not have his own radio or record player? In many homes one is likely to hear 'turn it down', or 'can't you live without that music on?', rather than requests for more sounds. Yet how many families make music together? How many even listen to the same music? One of the best solutions to the practical problem of the musical generation gap is to try from time to time to listen together to the same pieces, in order to discuss them and evaluate their merits together. We said in the first chapter that although music was omnipresent it tended to individualize people rather than unite them in real communion. One place where this process could begin to be reversed is the home.

It is important for families not only to listen to music together, but actually to *make* music together. Some musical instruments are quite easy to learn. The recorder can be bought cheaply, and mastered at least enough to be able to play some of the simplest literature. And recorder music is especially rewarding, as it can plunge the player into the world of the Renaissance. There are hundreds of duets and trios as well for those who can go a little further. And of course, the best (and easiest, at least to begin with) instrument of all is the human voice. Anyone can learn to sing, despite the popular slogans about tone-deafness. Christian families ought regularly to sing hymns after meals. It is quite an astonishing fact that Jesus and the disciples took the time to sing a hymn right after the last passover meal they shared together. One would have thought that with the impending distress of the betrayal and passion other things would be on their minds. But music had its place even at that terrible hour. In fact we might dare say it was a most important place, as it was the last activity Jesus and his disciples were to enjoy as a fellowship during his earthly ministry (Matt. 26.30). At any rate, if they found the time to sing, in those circumstances, we can hardly claim to be too busy to do likewise.

Travelling can be another occasion for family music-making. There is a considerable amount of folk music available in modern publications so that there should never be a lack of resources. It is surprising to discover the salutary effects of singing in the car when long miles are before the weary travellers. Entertaining guests at home is another occasion for music-making. This can be quite informal and impromptu. Or it could be organized into a musical soirée. Like parlour games, music is a means of bringing people together. And everybody wins!

A second realm to consider is music education. This is a broad field, which covers a good many different domains. It can include schools, the Church, musical criticism, television, and so on. Many governments are busy cutting back on budgets for the arts in public education, just at a time when they should be growing. Music is wrongly considered a luxury item, far more expendable than maths, languages, etc. But the opposite is true. Again, from what was said in the first chapter we may recall that the arts as a whole and music in particular are flourishing as never before in western societies. This has its problems, as we have seen. But the answer is surely not to educate our children and the public less in these areas.

For better or worse, schools have a more and more important role in the training of our children for every area of life. It may seem at first that such subjects as morality, athletics, the arts, should no more be inculcated at school than catechism. As the well-known music educator Dalcroze said in the earlier part of this century, 'It is evident that religion has ceased to inspire our teachers to preserve for musical studies the place they formerly occupied in the general education scheme.'[4] But his answer was to develop a method of music-learning which could be used in the schools, so that all would not be lost. His work was paralleled by others, like Carl Orff and Zoltán Kodály. In very different ways, each of these music educators discovered ways to communicate skills to children which were imaginative and practical. Dalcroze is best known for his 'eurythmics', a way of moving one's body to music which promotes awareness of the different components of musical texture. He found that using means such as walking to the pulse, clapping or throwing tennis balls to the accented beat, singing each melodic line, students became more 'musically co-ordinated'. Carl Orff used percussion instruments like the xylophone and the glockenspiel in the same way, showing children how to combine the movement of the arms and hands with pitch and rhythm. Kodály created a code for notes on the pentatonic scale with hand signals, thus enabling instructors to teach tunes in an efficacious way. While it is true that there are religious overtones to some of these approaches, especially the use of eurythmics, it is possible to use many of the particular methods effectively without bringing in what is essentially an oriental spirituality. Many schools in different countries have already adopted the methods of Dalcroze, Orff, Kodály and others. They are far more imaginative and interesting to children than the traditional listening to records for the music hour.

Among the many advantages of these suggestions is that they are more democratic than the prevailing systems in

110

many countries. In France, where I live, music education is essentially élitist. The national conservatory is a high-pressured academy which looks to promote the most gifted students, using the terrifying sorting-out procedure of judge and jury. The survivors go on to the next step, and eventually end up in Paris, where only the best are recruited. The sad result is that on the one hand musicians who make it through the system tend to be technically very competent, while lacking the maturity and confidence to become truly great musicians, while on the other hand hundreds of thousands of 'less gifted' students are ignored or left to fend for themselves, knowing that there will never be a place for them in the world of music. This sort of élitist approach is reinforced by radio and television programmes which idolize the young 'genius', the 'musician of the year', and so on, so that the public is under the impression that general musicianship is simply out of reach.

Here Christians can do a good deal to fight for a more balanced picture. One of the attractions of the electronic machines we discussed earlier is the relative ease with which certain effects can be produced. But here we can do our best to promote wider access to music-making without sacrificing quality or falling into an excessive use of technology. This will have to be a battle on several fronts, because we are dealing with more than just music education. We are dealing with radio and television programming. We are also dealing with the different copyright organizations which seem to be more and more powerful in western countries as time goes on.[5] In fact we are dealing with the whole system of patronage of the arts. Why are certain concerts backed by government money and not others? Why are some opera companies found worthy of state support and not others? The answer, of course, is in the people who are responsible for such designations. What are their criteria? Here it would be possible for Christians with a strong background in biblical aesthetics to have an impact.

A third consideration is the entertainment world. Understandably, many will hesitate to penetrate deep into this area of life, full as it is of temptations and pitfalls. Many Christians soon after their conversion find it incompatible with their spiritual goals to be a part of the world of entertainment. Yet

111

the abuses, which are very real, ought not to force us to ignore the opportunities. The word 'entertain' is a significant one. It originally meant to hold, then to take into service by hire. From this it came to mean to engage, or occupy attention in an agreeable way. The word also refers to receiving a guest, providing for his needs, giving him a meal. Naturally, music is a strong part of this engaging process. In the days of travel by horse and coach, when the roads were long and difficult, the traveller looked forward to staying at an inn where he could spend the night and be 'entertained'. Hospitality, wedding banquets, celebration, fellowship, all are a part of life as described in the New Testament, and there is nothing unspiritual about healthy entertainment.

One of the battles involved in keeping entertainment 'healthy' is in the development of the public's tastes. As art becomes available to more and more people through technical and economic means, it does not necessarily follow that aesthetic maturity and discerning judgement are promoted at the same rate. What often happens is that audiences become consumers of commercialized and sentimental sounds, or perhaps of the latest pop star pushed into the limelight through video-clips and other techniques. But then at the same time the way is opened to certain arbiters of public taste whose views are more élitist than conventionally authentic. An example of this sort of dichotomy can be drawn from the American scene at the beginning of the twentieth century. Most Americans at the time preferred listening to country and folk music, and to traditional hymns, such as those from the 'Sacred Harp' anthologies. But then some of the better-educated people discovered European high culture. They began to disparage the simpler styles of their heritage, and rather than patiently trying to educate the public toward a broadening of taste, they rejected folk music altogether. One statement can be taken as representative. It is made by a certain Theodore Thomas:

A symphony orchestra shows the culture of a community . . . The man who does not understand Beethoven and has not sat under his spell has not lived half his life. The master works of instrumental music are the language of the soul and express more than those of any other art. Light music, 'popular' so-called, is the sensual side of the art and has more or less the devil in it.[6]

This kind of attitude has contributed much to the present élitism we have been discussing. But it also tends to promote just the vulgarization and lowering of standards it decries, because it does not seek to grapple with folk music and other popular forms as genuinely worthy of musical criticism.

It has not often been appreciated that popular culture can be as genuine and authentic as the high culture promoted by élitists. Popular culture has helped people in mass society to develop their individuality, and to solve problems, as well as to enjoy themselves. Soap operas and Westerns have often portrayed family difficulties which could be solved by traditional morality. Popular music speaks of different moral dilemmas and ways to solve them. Home-making magazines suggest ways of decorating a dwelling space with a certain style, and within the budget of the users. Élitists tend to forget that much popular culture is in touch with its audience in a way that high culture is not. High culture tends to be in touch with the creators instead.[7] This is certainly true in music, where avant-garde music is so abstract that only the initiates can claim to understand it, and often only because they feel they ought to rather than because they enjoy it.

In saying this, we do not want to fall into the opposite danger, of romanticizing popular culture. There is great room for improvement there as well. When the market is going well, it is easy to fall into a kind of cultural laziness, and never move beyond what 'I like', as many frustrated church organists can affirm! Here the entertainer is in a crucial position. He is playing or singing what the audience wants to hear, presumably. But he also nurtures the audience's taste and desires. If his medium is the more popular one, say jazz or rock, he will constantly have to resist the temptation merely to be commercially successful and sensuously pleasing. If he is a 'classical musician' then he will not only have to deal with these temptations, but also with artistic snobbism. But in both cases the musician is doing what he can to 'till and keep' the world into which he is called. The environment is partly his responsibility, since he is called to fulfil the cultural

113

mandate to subdue the earth. Changing the environment takes a good deal of courage. But if we want to be faithful to God's call we shall have to show that courage even in the world of music.

Music in the Church

In many ways the church environment is like any other if one is called to make music in it. Yet there are special problems attached to this particular sphere of life. One reason is that biblical revelation specifies the nature and the elements of worship in a public gathering of the Church in quite definite terms. Not that Scripture tells us the hour of day to gather or even the order of the liturgy. But since Christianity is revealed religion, and since man's salvation depends entirely on how he comes to God, or, rather, how God comes to him, it follows that God cannot be worshipped in any way that strikes our fancy. This has been beautifully put in the Westminster Confession of Faith:

> God alone is Lord of the conscience, and hath left it free from the doctrines and commandments of men which are in any thing contrary to his word, or beside it, in matters of faith or worship. (XX. 2)

Imposing practices which are not authorized in Scripture runs the danger of destroying liberty. What a reversal of our usual modern logic, which has it that liberty is doing what we want! Put more negatively, but again emphasizing the central importance of worship, the Confession says this:

> But the acceptable way of worshipping the true God is instituted by himself, and so limited by his own revealed will, that he may not be worshipped according to the imaginations and devices of men, or the suggestions of Satan, under any visible representation, or any other way not prescribed in the holy scripture. (XXI. 1)

In a way, of course, the same could be said for all of life, not just worship. The point is that public worship is a high point in the believer's life, and it is full of biblical significance (Exod. 19.16–20; Ps. 50.4–6; 1 Cor. 11.17–34). And so the Church has often had to question certain practices and traditions to see if they were really 'prescribed in the holy scripture' or merely vain imaginations. This has meant great

114

controversy in the area of music, of course. The Protestant reformers, particularly the Swiss branch, were at times quite radical in their application of such a principle. Zwingli tended to avoid all music in church. Calvin favoured only unaccompanied Psalms, as we saw. But even Martin Luther, a great music-lover, was hesitant about many practices which he found in the late medieval Church, including the use of the organ.

The controversy was healthy as long as it did not fall into a sort of over-reaction to the Roman Catholic practices over against which the Reformation defined many of its positions. Over-reaction did at times set in, however. Sometimes it was overt. Sometimes it was clothed in terms of the need to appeal to the people. During the eighteenth century the Methodist Church was very concerned to avoid any kind of formalism, having been born of a reaction to the coldness of the official Church. This concern is echoed in its views of music. In the Minutes of the Conference of 1768, this concern is strongly expressed:

> Beware of formality in singing, or it will creep upon us unawares. 'Is it not creeping in already,' said they, 'by these complex tunes which it is scarcely possible to sing with devotion?' . . . The repeating the same word so often, as it shocks all common sense, so it necessarily brings in dead formality, and has no more religion in it than a Lancashire hornpipe.[8]

From this time on, many Evangelical Christians began to fear any music which did not have an immediate appeal. Of course, it was very important for the music of the revival periods to reach the people who were touched by the preaching. But at the same time a sort of reverse snobbism set in which eventually led to the defence of 'saccharine talents' in composers whose music was meant only to stir up the masses.[9] Anti-aestheticism in church music became synonymous with faithfulness to the 'simple gospel'. In fact it is a common observation of many modern Christians that where the Church is 'sound' the music will be mediocre, and where the music is beautiful, the Church will be 'liberal'.

The church musician has a vocation which obliges him to deal with this problem. He or she must help the congregation to become free from these false associations. Great tactfulness

115

will of course be essential. But also there are ways to help people grow out of a nostalgic sentimentalism and into greater spiritual, and therefore musical, maturity. People need to be shown the difference between the presence of feelings which remind them of worship, and true worship 'in Spirit and in truth' (John 4.24). This task is considerable. It will not be accomplished overnight. But it is important to realize that we are dealing with a spiritual problem, and not just a musicological one. It would be very gratifying if we could see some success here.

What Style?

I approach this subject with fear and trepidation. But it is unavoidable. The biblical principles which I have attempted to elucidate cannot be left without some application, or else the reader will tell me, in effect, that is all very well and good, but what do I do now? However, I fear many readers will be disappointed because I do not plan to give them ten easy rules for effective Christian music today! Not only would this be utterly pretentious, but it would also be inimical to those principles which I do think can be elaborated. Those involve patient work on the problems we face, living in our century, whether in music or in any other field, always with the realism, yet also the hope, of the biblical framework.

One of the first difficulties we face as modern Christians in the West is the choice of styles. Thanks to communications networks we are confronted with a dazzling array of possibilities. It is difficult even to put intelligent labels on the different types of musical styles available, let alone evaluate them. Even such seemingly clear categories as 'rock music' have sub-divisions which defy typology. And we do not really have any satisfactory terms for what is awkwardly called 'classical' or 'serious' music.

The picture may become a bit clearer when we realize that different styles can be observed to be cultivated and enjoyed by different social groups. A certain type of rock is listened to more frequently by people from one social background than others. For example, the sophisticated music of Bob Dylan, or even Pink Floyd, appeals to the upper-middle class white person, whereas the harder sounds of blues-oriented rock appeals more to the working class. Also, quite obviously, certain styles are deemed appropriate on certain occasions, while others are not. Few people will have ragtime played for their wedding march.

Another difficulty is cleared up when we begin to realize that the term 'style' is very ambiguous and not very helpful. Many people mistakenly think of style as clothing. That is, the content is clothed in a certain style. Thus, it is often assumed that a similar content can be translated into different styles, much as a person can change his or her attire. The problem is that in music, as the other arts as well, it is not possible to separate content from style. If you remove the style you have nothing left. Perhaps one could conceive of certain characteristics, like the rock beat or the baroque thorough-bass, as being stylistic features of a certain type of music. Thus one could conceivably write a baroque fugue with a rockish beat carried by the thorough-bass! But even there you would not have anything but a *hybrid style*. Perhaps it would be better simply to talk about certain conventions or types in the melodic and rhythmic structure of pieces of music. Then it would be possible to isolate stylistic elements more safely, and perhaps to reduce the number of them in a given period to a manageable number.

This would be an important step. If we are grasping after styles which are appropriate for our music-making, reducing the question to smaller units, bite-sized stylistic features, might help us face composition with less of a sense of depression at the mountain in front of us. Thus the pressure would be off to have to justify 'Christian rock', whatever that is. This is my problem with groups like Stryper and Barnabas in the United States, who play straight heavy-metal hard rock, and wear all of the paraphernalia, costumes adorned with chains and metal studs, but with one difference—the words sung are Christian. It is not that Christians cannot use style elements from rock music. But it is quite artificial to embrace an entire complex of style elements which were grown on the soil of the rebellious drug-and-sound culture of the late sixties, only changing the words (which are usually hard to make out anyway). This is the difficulty of writing music that is modern, yet free from certain connotations. James Ward's disco setting of Psalm 36, *Precious Is Your Mercy*, is more successful than the hard rock examples. The difficulty is in the view of culture as a receptacle. In a way this is saying that styles are neutral, only the core content is religiously specific. This would imply that style is like an apple or pear. Only the core needs to bear a message, the fleshy part is neutral. But a biblical view of style is very different. It is true that 'out of the heart come the issues of life', and so there are deep-seated places from which religious commitment emanates. But at the same time it is the entire person who is committed, body, soul, mind, strength. In this way 'style is the man', as one philosopher has said.

This does not mean that style is an after-thought. The problem of determining a musical style for a given work, or even as the chosen medium for a period of time in one's compositional life, is similar to choices we make in other areas, like the furniture in a room, the tone of a conversation, the shape of a garden. Because music is a symbolical cultural activity the choice of style will have to be even more self-conscious than in these cases.

Communication

Let us come to a few specifics. I would like to propose the consideration of two principles which might guide us in the choice of styles. The first is communication. No composer, no listener, can ignore the importance of communication. Although music is not propaganda, as we have stressed, it is deeply involved with communication on many different levels. Stylistic elements are a function of communication. Because the content of what is communicated can be extremely broad and varied, the choices of stylistic elements will be as well.

An example of the breadth of what is involved could be taken from one of Stravinsky's religious works, the *Mass*, written in 1948. It is scored for mixed chorus (soprano and alto parts preferably sung by boys), and a double wind quintet (five woodwinds and five brass). It is a standard Ordinary in five sections. Although it only takes seventeen minutes to perform, the compositional features are quite involved. It is a work destined for liturgical purposes. This already marks off a certain number of parameters. Quite deliberately, the general effect of the piece is that of the traditional Masses from the medieval period. The *Ars Nova* techniques of Guillaume de Machaut are strongly in evidence.

118

This too puts us very much in the setting of the Church, with its liturgical tradition.

Stravinsky disliked the pretentious sounds of rococo opera, and he deliberately streamlined the *Mass*, so as to put the listener into a certain frame of reverence. The instrumental background of simple, slowly-modulating chordal patterns highlights the straightforward declamation of the voices. The homophony of the chorus sets the tone for prayer and personal participation. What we might recognize as distinctly modern features, like the dissonances used to outline certain chords and the unusual, at times exotic, instrumentation, is convincingly integrated into the whole. In other words they do not draw attention to themselves.

It is possible to detect certain theological emphases, in spite of the uniformity and apparently unemotional style. A brief instrumental commentary highlights the central aspects of the *Credo*, such as the *homo factus est*. But all is in its place, in continuity with tradition. We are light years away from the treatment of the *Credo* by Beethoven or Verdi, where the passion of Christ is underscored, and the extravagant musical texture invites the listener into a world where theology and human emotion are fused together. In the Stravinsky, we are humble participants in an eternal truth which is situated far above our subjective relation to it. The choice of stylistic elements is altogether appropriate.

The problem of style should not be one of whether to choose innovative rather than traditional forms. Because of his attention to his musical heritage Stravinsky has often been called 'neo-classical'. While is it true that certain modern composers have turned in a rather artificial way to the past, in their search for ways to renew their art, the type of connection which Stravinsky espoused in the *Mass* is far deeper. Communication is not possible if there is no continuity with the art of the past. This is so because human beings do not operate in a vacuum. It is especially true for Christians, who stand in continuity with the historic Church. At the same time, this frees us to be really modern. Once we are free from the tyranny of the novel, we can become comfortable in the languages of today. Francis Schaeffer comments on this:

First, Christian art today should be twentieth-century art. Art changes. Language changes. The preacher's preaching today must be twentieth-century language communication, or there will be an obstacle to being understood. And if a Christian's art is not twentieth-century art, it is an obstacle to his being heard. It makes him different in a way in which there is no necessity for difference. A Christian should not, therefore, strive to copy Rembrandt or Browning.[10]

The principle of communication has another dimension which should not be neglected. We could call it indigenous authenticity. By that is meant stylistic adaptation to the particular paradigmatic, moral and social context in which one is operating. The matter of indigenous authenticity comes up both at home and abroad. One of the places where its features have been most dramatically needed is the so-called mission field. Mistakes have been made. In some cases Anglican hymns have been imposed on cultures which are quite foreign to its style. In others the opposite effect from what was desired has been produced, such as evoking sadness instead of joy through a rapid beat. While there is no doubt that certain cultural norms, including musical ones, will have to be challenged, because they are at conflict with covenant principles, there may also be much that can be incorporated, and turned into the 'new song'.

This process has actually occurred in a number of societies which have been confronted with the gospel. In the Polynesian islands there is a group called the Kingdom of Tonga. It is an interesting place, because it came into modernity without becoming a colony of a western power, as most of its neighbours did. In the previous century the entire group accepted Christianity, and put their traditional polytheistic practices behind them. During the time that immediately followed their conversion it seemed important to suppress certain types of singing and dance which powerfully signified pagan worship. But then a body of Christian hymns was gradually developed, called *hiva fakahokohoko'ofa*, which used and adapted pre-Christian choral music, making certain changes, leading to a kind of style that is definitely indigenous, yet without being 'neo-classical'. This has meant a great freedom in worship for the people of those islands: 'When the congregation hears a person(s) beginning to feel a spiritual

120

warmth they begin a series of these songs to help maintain the feeling. The music helps people to unlock their hearts and give full expression to their feelings of belief and closeness to God.'[11]

Incarnation

The second principle in the choice of styles is something like naturalness. Without wanting to be guilty of effrontery, we can find a certain analogy between the Incarnation of our Lord, the Word made flesh, and the creative process. For a piece of music to be 'natural' the choice of style must not only *correspond* with the needs of the composition, but must in a way be *wedded* to them. The form and content must come together into a unity. In this way stylistic elements are not simply chosen in an artificial way. They are a function of other choices, those which govern the entire compositional process. When this wedding is absent, we find something missing in the piece, we find a conflict between intentions and realization.

A possible example of this is Arnold Schönberg's *Quartet for Strings, No. 4*, Opus 37. The stylistic convention of twelve-note or twelve-tone writing is one of its structural features. The first movement begins with an exposition of a note-row (or tone-row) in the first violin:

The doctrine of dodecaphonic writing dictates that no previous notes may be used until all twelve have been set down. Against this universalistic principle it seems that Schönberg felt the need to pull in another direction. In order to 'humanize' the abstract principle, he does two things. First, he converts the row into a melodic form, giving it certain rhythmic features.

In doing this he borrows from the more lyrical tradition of string quartet melody. He resists the tendency to serialize all the parameters as Boulez would later do. The second thing is to use the accompanying parts in a dance-like pattern. While the rhythm is supple, the twelve-note principle is still respected, because all the notes of the row are distributed among the three lower voices, and used up in each bar (measure).

There is a kind of conflict here between two intentions. The rich warmth of the content is not fully incarnate in the rigidity of the twelve-tone approach. This raises the question of whether it is ever possible to use twelve-note principles in an incarnational way. Can Christians, in their legitimate desire to be modern, take this particular stylistic innovation, isolate it from its modernist orthodoxy, and place it in a more 'redeemed' setting? It is hard to be categorical here. The difficulty is not so much with the idea of non-tonal music, nor is it with the use of numbers. It is with the narrow way in which we are asked to engage in the dodecaphonic system as an all-encompassing style.

Twelve-note writing is not the only modern style which poses problems. The minimalist school of more recent times raises the same difficulty. Composers like Tibor Szemzo, Steve Reich and Laszlo Melis have set forth a style which exploits the very smallest musical elements. The idea is to contemplate one particular melodic or harmonic aspect in an exhaustive way. Steve Reich's *Music for Pieces of Wood* (1973) is built on the model of a mobile. Scored for the claves, a simple percussion instrument, the work is organized around metrical units of 6/4, 4/4 and 3/4. Each section of the piece explores a different combination of these units as they complement each other. The listener is subjected to various permutations without any apparent direction. Drawn to certain Eastern philosophies, the minimalist composers seek to permeate the atmosphere with simple sound combinations, much as colour variations can be experienced through the kaleidoscope. But the pieces lack depth and organic development. Can some of these compositional devices be used without limiting the music in such a way?

The solution, it seems to me, is to be modern without being modernist. That is, a modern preoccupation for shapes, forms and numbers can be perfectly well explored without falling into an all-encompassing system. This is in line with what was said earlier about style being flexible and not englobing. One of the most successful modern composers, in this sense, is Olivier Messiaen (1908—   ). He is fascinated by all kinds of musical and extra-musical properties. He is the inventor of 'les modes à transpositions limités', a series of scales contained within the twelve chromatic notes of the

123

tempered system. Using groupings based on the divisors 2, 3, 4 and 6, he found that seven different combinations were possible. His favourite were the second and third:

His interest in these modes was not for their religious value, contrary to what is often affirmed about his connections with Indian raga music. He wanted to experiment with various sound qualities. He derived chords from these modes. He sought to discover different harmonic values from the intervals. He also experimented with timbre in relation to harmony. One frequently-used technique is what he called 'added resonance'. Different features of harmonic qualities come into prominence when they are orchestrated in a certain way. The following example from his *Couleurs de la Cité Céleste* shows how he goes about it.

The quiet chord in the higher clarinets resonates in a special way with the triple forte of the low-register brass instruments, filling out the harmonic colour in a resonating way.

One of Messiaen's greatest works is *Quatuor Pour la Fin du Temps — Quartet for the End of Time —* (1941). Written in a German prison camp, the work reflects the circumstances, but not in an expected way. In his *stalag* there happened to be a violinist, a 'cellist and a clarinetist. In spite of the cold and hunger, he managed to compose a work which reflects not the apocalyptic catastrophe of war but the eternal state. He plays with the idea of the reversibility and invertibility of rhythms. Full of mathematical puzzles as it is, we never have the impression of coldness. On the contrary, it is a superbly musical work. In the first section, called *Liturgy of Crystal*, he manages to blend together four very different 'protagonists', four instruments, each one realizing a specific rhythmic-melodic motif, including the remarkable clarinet part or voice . which is partly meant to imitate bird sounds:

The other parts are doing equally idiomatic things, yet taken together there is a sense of collective improvisation. Here again, the stylistic elements are modern, but they are used for the larger purpose of incarnation.

The same principle applies to formal organization as well. Style is also a function of the overall form of a piece. Although no rule exists which guarantees success, certain guidelines can be observed. Again, there are so many different kinds of pieces, so many formal options, that we shall simply have to look at one or two examples. In contrast to some of the extravagant orchestral works of the nineteenth century, modern composers have often been concerned to use sparse materials. Conciseness is a governing quality of Stravinsky's *Agon*, a ballet in several movements, first performed in 1957. The opening Pas-de-quatre is scored for a large orchestra, yet the musical material is rudimentary. It consists of three motifs, which are as follows:

The movement is 60 bars long, and its basic tonality is C major. What is of interest is the way in which the motifs are held together, and developed within the limits of this framework. The pulse is regular and conveys a strong metronome sense. The structure of the whole is divided into four parts with roughly the same shape and length. The first part sets up the standard pattern which the three others depend upon. An expectation is thus established, and the rest of the piece builds on it. The entire movement looks like this, in outline form:

	Bars	1 – 3	4 – 6	7 – 9	10 – 12	12 + 13
I	Motifs	A	B	S	C	Cadence

II	14–18	19–22	23–25	26–29
	B^1	S	C	C^1

III	30–31	32–34	35–38	39–42	43–45
	A^1	B^{11}	S^1	C^1	liquid material following C

IV	46–53	54–60	(59)	60
	$A^{11} + B^{111}$	C → subdivision of C	Final cadence

Each motif is somewhat varied in the successive sections. One device which serves as a special propelling device, a sort of way to say: 'the piece will now move forward', is what I have called S. It is a signal, consisting of two parts, the outline of an open C chord in long notes by the high woodwinds and horns, and short triplets in the lower strings:

The effect of this signal is to push the piece forward, onto the second half of the section. In the fourth and last section, the signal is absent, and in its place we have motif C, then cadential material, and the end.

To receive the full impact it is important to listen to the piece rather than analyse it in the abstract. Stravinsky's stylistic choices, which include open diatonic sounds, unusual timbre contrasts, regular pulsation, are integrated into an overall form which permits them to live together organically. The form actually suggests the content.

Beyond Style

In the craft of music-making there is another ingredient which is difficult to pin down. It is more than just the successful implementation of stylistic elements. It is a quality which begins in the soul of the composer. One could call it authenticity, although the term is a stereotype. Identification of this kind of genuineness is somewhat subjective, and I do not want to suggest anything particularly mysterious, so perhaps we can be content simply to think of it in terms of authenticity in other areas. Just as a person may have strong integrity in his behaviour, so he might display the same qualities in his art.

A comparison between two pieces from the field of jazz will help us be more specific. Limiting the terrain of contrasts, let us take two piano waltzes, written by two well-known jazz musicians. The first is *Waltz for Debby*, by Bill Evans. It is built on a series of chord progressions which are quite classical in feeling:

It is delicate, even pretty. It has qualities that remind of Chopin, including an interlude which is quite Romantic. But somehow it lacks the quality of a jazz piece. It lacks drive, or as jazz musicians might say, it doesn't *swing*. It is a lovely jewel, but stands outside of the tradition of black American music.

In contrast, we can look at Erroll Garner's *Nervous Waltz*. The overall structure of the piece is not very different from the first waltz. Yet the total effect is very different.

The way the chords are voiced gives a much rougher, gutsy sound. The melody is at the same time more clearly delineated than in the Evans piece, and also less 'pretty'. The stress on the first two of three beats puts tension into the work. These features are far more clear in the performance than in the score, of course. The overall effect of the Evans piece is one of jazz conventions used for a lovely waltz, whereas with the Garner there is an element of authenticity that comes through the roughness.

Erroll Garner stands in the tradition of black American music, whose history goes back to the times when the hymns of Wesley and Watts were transformed by the slaves into negro spirituals. These spirituals in turn were the source of the blues and jazz. Black Americans in slavery were not concerned with stylistic questions in an academic way. Yet their experience was the fundamental reason for their creative process. Taking what was available, Puritan hymns, baroque dance suites, their West African recollections, they worked with them from the standpoint of their experience with the life of slavery, informed by the hope of the gospel. As their character was being forged on this anvil, the 'new song' arose, in all of its authenticity.

A fascinating account of how this happened can be an eye-opener on this process. The ex-slave Jeanette Robinson Murphy gave her impressions to a chronicler. With apologies for the racist transcription, part of it is reproduced here:

> We'd all be at the 'prayer house' de Lord's day, and de white preacher he'd splain de word and read what Esekial done say —
> *Dry bones gwine ter lib ergin.*
> And, honey, de Lord would come a-shinin' thoo dem pages and revive dis ole nigger's heart, and I'd jump up dar and den and holler and shout and sing and pat, and dey would all cotch de words and I'd sing it to some ole shout song I'd heard 'em sing from Africa, and dey'd all take it up and keep at it, and keep a-addin' to it, and den it would be a spiritual.[12]

Here we have the incarnate bond between the content (the message of Ezekiel) and the form (hollers, songs from Africa, etc.), based on the experience of the believing soul. It is this combination which can give 'the new song'.

131

Concluding Unmusical Postscript

It may come as some surprise to learn that the great Christian author C. S. Lewis never started one of his fictional works with a message. Nor did he preoccupy himself very much with what kind of style or genre to adopt. In a fascinating interview with Kingsley Amis, published posthumously in 1965, C. S. Lewis discusses his writing method. What is particularly significant is the relation between the subject matter and the content of the writings, and the way in which they come into being:

> The starting point of the second novel, *Perelandra*, was my mental picture of the floating islands. The whole of the rest of my labours in a sense consisted of building up a world in which floating islands could exist. And then of course the story about an averted fall developed. This is because, as you know, having got your people to this exciting country, something must happen.[13]

What Lewis is underscoring here is that it is probably not a good idea to begin with a message, and then look around for a way to put it. That would be fine on some occasions, of course, just as composing chant for Psalm recitals in church must necessarily begin with the message. But usually 'having something to say' first and then finding the proper medium leads to propaganda art. It also leads us to forget that the arts are human, cultural response, involving aesthetic dominion over the world. It is best to leave pure message-bearing to preachers, scientists, and moralists, who are called to say things more directly. As someone once said, the best authors have blood running in their veins, not ink.

Our calling, then, is to go back into our world, armed with these biblical principles, and to make it a more fit dwelling place for humankind. We can do this because we have been bought with a price, and the power of Christ is in us. We make melody in our heart because fellowship with our Lord causes us to sing. The ultimate source of this calling is God himself, who is already at work to change the landscape of this world from one of sorrow and tears to one of great beauty:

> For the Lord will comfort Zion;
> he will comfort all her waste places,

and will make her wilderness like Eden,
    her desert like the garden of the Lord;
joy and gladness will be found in her,
    thanksgiving and the voice of the song (Isa. 51.3).

Making the earth into a beautiful place. This is our high calling. It is not a utopian programme nor is it one more social platform for improvement. We are called instead to 'show forth the excellencies of him who called you out of darkness into his marvellous light' (1 Pet. 2.9, ASV). These excellencies include the strange glory of a God who was willing to subject himself to suffering and death. Jesus Christ, hanging on the cross, 'had no form or comeliness that we should look at him, and no beauty that we should desire him' (Isa. 53.2). And yet at that moment he was beauty itself, lifted up high, to draw all men to himself (John 12.32).

This is why it is that the experience of beauty, whether in visual art, in literature or in music, is deeply related to ultimate reality, to God's presence and to his plan for us: 'Here as in worship, in love, in moral action, and in knowing, I transcend myself; and I am never more myself than when I do.'14 We sing to God because he first sang to us (Zeph. 3.17). How utterly more exquisite than the music of the morning stars must God's song be.

Notes

Chapter 1

1. Lesschaeve, Jacqueline, *The Dancer and the Dance*. New York, Marion Boyars, 1985.
2. Ahlstrom, D., 'Furnishing Music: An Analysis of Mass Media Music in Terms of Music Systems' (*Arts in Society* XII/2, 1975), pp. 248—56.
3. Russolo, Luigi, 'Manifeste futuriste', 11 mars 1913 (*L'art des bruits*, Paris, L'age d'homme, 1975), pp. 35—43.
4. Taruskin, Richard, 'Some Thoughts on the History and Historiography of Russian Music' (*The Journal of Musicology* III/4, 1984), p. 323.
5. Starr, S. Frederick, *Red and Hot: The Fate of Jazz in the Soviet Union* (New York, Oxford University Press, 1983), pp. 318—19.
6. The technical term for this learning is 'bi-musicality'. The best-known advocate of this kind of international music appreciation is ethnomusicologist Mantle Hood. His view is contested by some who believe it is impossible to enter the mind-set of people from other cultures.
7. Finson, Jon, 'Music and Medium: Two Versions of Manilow's "Could It Be Magic?"' (*The Musical Quarterly* LXV/2, 1979), pp. 265—80.
8. Barrett, William, *The Illusion of Technique: A Search for Meaning in a Technological Civilization* (Garden City NJ, Anchor Books, 1978), pp. 307—10.
9. Wallis, Roger and Malm, Krister, *Big Sounds from Small People: The Music Industry in Small Countries*. London, Constable, 1984.
10. Lang, Paul Henry, *Music in Western Civilization* (New York, Norton, 1941), p. 1007.
11. Webern, Anton von, *The Path to the New Music, 1932—33* (Bryn Mawr Pa, Theodore Presser, 1963), p. 54.

Chapter 2

1. Guterboch, H. G., 'Musical Notation in Ugarit' (*Revue d'Assyriologie* LVIV, 1970), p. 47.
2. The expression 'partakers of the divine nature' in 2 Peter 1.4 is not what it seems, a confusion between created and uncreated essence. Neither is it a blending into the Godhead by creatures. The context indicates an ethical reference. It is basically a

moral likeness to God's righteousness; not a commingling of essence, but '*koinonia*' with the divine '*phusis*'. Even in Thomas Aquinas's theology, which emphasizes this biblical text, the concept is never one of a metaphysical 'migration' into God's being.

3. See Berkouwer, G. C., *General Revelation* (Grand Rapids Mi., Eerdmans, 1955), pp. 131—2.

4. Rameau, J. -P., *Observations sur notre instinct pour la musique et sur son principe.* 1754. For a similar view, from outside Western culture, see Powers, William K., 'Oglala Song Terminology' (*Selected Reports in Ethnomusicology* III/2, 1980), pp. 23—41.

5. Rousseau, J. -J., *Lettre sur la musique française.* 1753. Rameau's and Rousseau's particular views of nature differed in that the former stressed the harmony of the natural order, while the latter believed in the 'order' of uncorrupted *human* nature.

6. See Reese, Gustave, *Music in the Middle Ages*, New York, Norton, 1940; Schrade, Leo, 'The Chronology of the Ars Nova in France' (*Les Colloques de Wégimont II, 1955* (Paris 1959)). pp. 139—48; and de Bruyne, E., *The Esthetics of the Middle Ages.* New York 1969.

7. Leichtentritt, Hugo, 'The Gothic Period', in William Hays, ed., *Twentieth-Century Views of Music History* (New York, Scribner's, 1972), p. 65.

8. Keil, C. F., *Biblical Commentary on the Old Testament* Vol I, The Pentateuch (Grand Rapids Mi., Eerdmans), pp. 109—11.

9. See Kline, Meredith, *Images of the Spirit* (Grand Rapids Mi., Baker Books, 1980), pp. 20—1.

10. The introductory phrase, 'These are the generations of . . .' (Gen. 2.4), makes it clear that we are dealing with a focus on man in the garden, the fall into sin, and other specifics, not with a (contradictory) second version of the creation story. The introductory expression occurs ten times in the Book of Genesis and is an important factor in the structure of the book.

11. Kroeber, A. L., *Anthropology: Culture Patterns and Processes* (San Diego, New York, London, Harcourt Brace Jovanovich, 1948, 1963), p. 61.

12. Clowney, Edmund P., 'Interpreting the Biblical Models of the Church' in Carson, D. A., ed., *Biblical Interpretation and the Church: The Problem of Contextualization* (Nashville Tn, Thomas Nelson, 1985), p. 68.

13. See, for example, Wagner, Roy, *The Invention of Culture* (Chicago & London, University of Chicago Press, 1981), pp. 38—40, 62.

14. Conn, Harvie, 'Conversion and Culture', in Stott, John R. W.

and Coote, Robert, eds., *Down to Earth: Studies in Christianity and Culture* (Grand Rapids Mi., Eerdmans, 1980), p. 149.

15. Bavinck, J. H., *The Impact of Christianity on the Non-Christian World* (Grand Rapids Mi., Eerdmans, 1949), p. 57.

16. Steck, O. H., *Die Paradieserzählung* (Biblische Studien 60). Neukirchen, Neukirchener Verlag, 1970.

17. Kline, Meredith, op. cit., p 17.

18. ibid., p. 89.

19. Karl Barth's exegesis that the image of God involves maleness and femaleness is intriguing, especially as both Genesis 1.27 and 5.2 seem to connect it with the two sexes. However the link is far clearer with what comes after, not before, so that the possibility of reproduction in order to fulfil the dominion-mandate is explained by male and female. 1 Corinthians 11.7ff. is a most difficult text, but it cannot be derived from it that men are superior to women. The implication is rather that if woman is the glory of man, then 'humankind', both male and female, is the glory of God. It is not a passage about the ontology of the image of God.

20. Herndon, Marcia and McLeod, Norma, *Music As Culture* (Norwood Pa., Norwood Editions, 1979 rev. 1981), pp. 6—7.

21. Merriam, Alan, *The Anthropology of Music* (Evanston Il., Northwestern University Press, 1964), p. 27.

22. A helpful discussion of culture, in terms of the problems of relativism, in the light of paradigmatic structure, is in Conn, Harvie M., *Eternal Word and Changing Worlds* (Grand Rapids Mi., Zondervan, 1984), pp. 315—20.

Chapter 3

1. Boulez, Pierre, *Penser la musique aujourd'hui* (Paris, Gouthier, 1963), pp. 24—31.

2. ibid., p. 35.

3. Boulez, Pierre, 'Auprès et au loin' in *La musique et ses problèmes contemporains, 1953—1963* (Paris, René Julliard, 1963), pp. 14—15.

4. Stravinsky, Igor, *An Autobiography* (New York, Norton, 1962), pp. 161—4.

5. ibid., pp. 53—4.

6. Quoted in Griffiths, Paul, *A Concise History of Avant-Garde Music from Debussy to Boulez* (New York & Toronto. Oxford University Press, 1978), p. 129.

7. Quoted in Palmer, Robert, *Deep Blues* (London, Macmillan, 1981), p. 85.

8. Powers, Harold, 'Language Models and Musical Analysis' (*Ethnomusicology* XXIV/1, 1980), pp. 3—7.

9. ibid., p. 38.
10. See Nettl, Bruno, 'The State of Research in Ethnomusicology, and Recent Developments' (*Current Musicology* XX, 1975), pp. 67—78.
11. Feld, Steve, 'Linguistics and Ethnomusicology' (*Ethnomusicology* XVIII, 1974), pp. 197—217. Also Boretz, Benjamin, 'Meta-Variations: Studies in the Foundations of Musical Thought' (*Perspectives of New Music* VIII, 1969), pp. 51ff.
12. Quoted in a review of the Norton Lectures, by Hightower, Marvin, 'The Linguistics of Music' (*Genesis* II, 1976), p. 27. A similar approach is espoused by Cooke, Deryck, *The Language of Music*. Oxford, Oxford University Press, 1960.
13. The term is from Wolterstorff, Nicholas, *Art in Action* (Grand Rapids Mi., Eerdmans, 1980), pp. 114ff.
14. Powers, Harold, op. cit., p. 28.
15. Meyer, Leonard B., *Emotion and Meaning in Music* (Chicago, University of Chicago Press, 1956), p. 5.
16. ibid., pp. 5—6.
17. Meyer, Leonard B., 'Some Remarks on Value and Greatness in Music' in Phillipson, M., ed., *Aesthetics Today* (Cleveland & New York, Meridian Books, 1961), pp. 169—87.
18. Diderot, Denis, *Lettre sur les sourds et les muets*. Paris 1746.
19. Ricoeur, Paul, *La métaphore vive* (Paris, Le Seuil, 1975), p. 307.
20. Langer, Susanne K., *Feeling and Form* (New York, Scribner's, 1953), p. 126.
21. Brenneis, Donald, 'Passion and Performance in Fiji Indian Vernacular' (*Ethnomusicology* XXIX/3, 1985), p. 405.
22. *Der vollkommene Cappelmeister*. Hamburg 1739.
23. Dylan, Bob, 'Man Gave Names to all the Animals' from *Slow Train Coming*, CBS Inc., 1979.
24. See Chaplin, Adrienne, 'Music and Meaning', seminar outline for London Institute for Contemporary Christianity Music Conference, 12 January 1985.
25. Haar, James, 'Music History and Cultural History' (*Journal of Musicology* I/1, 1982), p. 13.

Chapter 4
1. This information, along with some of what follows, is drawn from Starr, S. Frederick, *Red and Hot: The Fate of Jazz in the Soviet Union* (New York, Oxford University Press, 1983), see pp. 83ff.
2. ibid., p. 85.
3. Rookmaaker, Hans R., *Modern Art and the Death of a Culture* (Downers Grove Il., Inter-Varsity Press, 1970), p. 30.

4. See Davies, Horton, *Worship and Theology in England* Vol. III (Princeton, Princeton University Press, 1961), p. 272.

5. The 'Epistre au lecteur' was first published in the *Liturgy of 1542*, and thereafter appears only in the psalters. For a translation, see Strunk, Oliver, *Source Readings in Music History* (New York, Norton, 1965), pp. 155–8.

6. ibid., p. 158.

7. 'So I waver between the danger that lies in gratifying the senses and benefits which, as I know from experience, can accrue from singing. Without committing myself to an irrevocable opinion, I am inclined to approve of the custom of singing in church, in order that by indulging the ears weaker spirits may be inspired with feelings of devotion. Yet when I find the singing itself more moving than the truth which it conveys, I confess that this is a grievous sin, and at those times I would prefer not to hear the singer.' (*The Confessions* X.33).

8. op. cit., p. 157.

9. Especially in *Book III*.

10. *Institutes of the Christian Religion* III. xx. 32.

11. See McKinnon, James, 'The Church Fathers and Musical Instruments', Unpublished Doctoral Thesis, Columbia University, New York 1965.

12. Quoted in Scholes, Percy A., *The Puritans and Music in England and New England* (Oxford, Oxford University Press, 1934), p. 352.

13. Régimbal, Jean-Paul, et al., *Le Rock N' Roll* [*sic*]*, viol de la conscience par les messages subliminaux*. Geneva, Editions Croisade, 1983.

14. Gore, Mrs Albert, et al., *Rock Music Report* (Washington, unpublished document, June 1985), p. 2.

15. Prince, 'Darling Nikki' from *Purple Rain*, Warner Bros., 1983.

16. Harrer, G. and H., 'Music, Emotion and Automatic Function', in Critchley, M. and Henson, R. A., eds., *Music and the Brain* (London, Heinemann Medical Books, 1977), pp. 202–16. This is confirmed by Zwang, D., see Simonis, Pierre, 'Les messages subliminaux' (*Ichthus* CXXVII/8, 1984), p. 19.

17. Paris, Gallimard 1980.

18. ibid., pp. 26–38.

19. See Belo, Jane, *Trance in Bali* (New York, Columbia University Press, 1960), pp. 201–25.

20. Needham, Rodney, 'Percussion and Transition' (*Man* (N.S.) II, 1967), pp. 606–14.

21. See Neher, Andrew, 'A Physiological Explanation of Unusual Behavior in Ceremonies Involving Drums' (*Human Biology* IV, 1962), pp. 151–60.

22. Rouget, op. cit., p. 252.
23. The expression is Rouget's, ibid., p. 241.
24. ibid., pp. 144, 178, 263, 408.
25. ibid., p. 180.
26. In a recent publication in China, *How To Distinguish Decadent Songs*, various western musical 'perversions' are described: jazz is syncopated music that 'forces people to accept what is unexpected, the abnormal beat', and 'dancing to this kind of music is like having nervous spasms', because 'the rhythm of jazz is against the normal psychological needs of man'. Similarly rock has a 'frenzied beat, neighing-like singing', and the percussion is 'intense to provoke the nerves'. None of this type of popular music has any artistic value, but 'it meets the needs of the people's negative spiritual life in capitalist society'. In the West, music critics like David Noebel have seen a communist conspiracy using rock music to infiltrate and incite to rebellion. It's hard to win, here!
27. Madonna, 'Material Girl' from *Like a Virgin*, Sire Records, 1984/85.
28. Rouget has an interesting view of our passage. He refutes the idea of magic also. Neither is it a case of exorcism, he says. He tries to show (unsuccessfully, I think) that David's music was connected with the trance, either to bring God's Spirit back to Saul, or to bring him out of an obsessive trance. David thus would have brought him back to reality (which I agree with), and to Saul's prophetic office (as in 1 Sam. 10.5−6) by substituting one spirit for another (which I disagree with−there is no evidence in the text for such a transfer). Rouget in fact does not seem to believe in the existence of spirits. See op. cit., p. 229.
29. The Canons of Dordt remind us that God's grace is 'irresistible' if God decides to save us. But this is not the same level of divine-human interaction involved in our response to the word of God. It is quite obviously possible to resist even God's Spirit, in the sinful exercise of free agency (see Matt. 12.31−2).
30. There is a fine discussion of the problem in Berkouwer, G. C., *Sin* (Grand Rapids Mi., Eerdmans, 1971).
31. 'I felt I was no longer free'.
32. Rookmaaker, H. R., *Modern Art and the Death of a Culture*, op. cit., p. 107.
33. Webern, Anton von, *The Path to the New Music*. Bryn Mawr Pa., Theodore Presser, 1963.
34. ibid., p. 36.
35. ibid., p. 56.
36. ibid., p. 54. We have already commented on the double meaning

behind the word 'salvation' for Webern.

37. Malraux, André, *Les voix du silence*. Paris, La Pléiade, 1951.

38. Actually in France, where I live, the state-operated radio stations are broadcasting more and more avant-garde music, especially by composers from the state-funded IRCAM centre at the Centre Pompidou, a seed-bed of electronics pantheism.

Chapter 5

1. See L'Engle, Madeleine, *Walking on Water: Reflections on Faith and Art* (Wheaton Il., Harold Shaw, 1980), pp. 179f.

2. Calvin, John, *Commentary on the First Book of Moses Called Genesis*. Grand Rapids Mi., Eerdmans, 1852.

3. Vos, Geerhardus, *The Kingdom of God and the Church* (Phillipsburg, NJ, Presbyterian and Reformed, 1979), pp. 88—9.

4. Jacques-Dalcroze, Emile, *Rhythm, Music and Education* (Geneva, Dalcroze Society, 1967), p. 7.

5. A somewhat alarmist but fairly accurate account of the way musical creativity can be stifled through élitism and centralization is Joseph, Jean-Pierre, *Le Show Business Français: Un état dans l'Etat*. Grenoble, Les Cahiers de la Pensée Sauvage, 1984.

6. Quoted in Leonard, Neil, *Jazz and the White Americans* (Chicago, University of Chicago Press, 1962), p. 16.

7. See Gans, Herbert J., *Popular Culture and High Culture* (New York, Basic Books, 1974), pp. 55—64.

8. Quoted in Reynolds, W. J., *A Survey of Christian Hymnody* (New York, Holt, Rinehart and Winston, 1963), p. 57. This attitude was carried on to the 'mission field', where indigenous sounds were often suppressed because they were said to associate too closely with pagan connotations.

9. ibid., p. 67.

10. Schaeffer, Francis A., *Art and the Bible* (Downers Grove Il., Inter-Varsity Press, 1973), p. 51.

11. Shumway, Larry V., 'The Tongan *Lakalala*: Music Composition and Style' (*Ethnomusicology* XXV/3, 1981), p. 471. This is probably what was happening at the time of the Reformation with practices such as the *contrafacta* which substituted one text for another, and modified certain musical details as well. The modifications were fewer and less radical than what we find on the 'mission field', because the cultural tradition of the Reformers was basically the same as that of the institutions they were trying to renew.

12. From 'The Survival of African Music in America' (*Popular Science Monthly* LV, 1899), pp. 660—72, as quoted in Jackson,

B., ed., *The Negro and His Folklore in Nineteenth Century Periodicals* (Austin Tx., 1967), p. 328.
13. 'Unreal Estates: On Science Fiction' (*Encounter* XXIV/3, 1965), p. 62.
14. Lewis, C. S., *An Experiment in Criticism* (Cambridge, Cambridge University Press, 1961), p. 141.

Index

Abel *see* Cain and Abel
Amis, Kingsley 132
Ansermet, Ernest 16
Aquinas, Thomas 135
Arabic music 5, 67
Aristotle 64, 74
Armstrong, Louis 5
Augustine 82

Bach, Johann Sebastian 13,
    21, 30, 61, 72, 77
Barnabas 117
Basie, William 'Count' 14
Bavinck, J. H. 39, 136
Beecham, Sir Thomas 16
Beethoven, Ludwig 5, 7,
    14, 58, 71-2, 112, 119
Berlioz, Hector 72
Bernstein, Leonard 61-2
Bible and music 1-2, ch. 2
    passim, 58, 65-6, 68-70,
    79-80, 99-108, 114
black American music 20,
    57, 84, 129, 131
blues 57-8, 60, 90, 116,
    131
Boulez, Pierre 53-4, 73,
    122, 136
Bowie, David 9
Brahms, Johannes 5
Breil, Joseph Carl 4

Cage, John 56-7

Cain and Abel 23-6, 34-5
calling 102-8, 132-3
Calvin, John 81-3, 105,
    115, 140
Cézanne, Paul 73
Charles, Ray 20
Chomsky, Noam 61-2
Chopin, Frédéric 17, 129
Christ, Jesus 29, 33, 35,
    42, 68, 75, 92, 102-9,
    121, 132-3
Church 15, 20, 22, 32, 77,
    102-9, 114-16, 119
Church Fathers 83, 138
Clapton, Eric 9
Couperin, François 72
Croft, William 63
cultural mandate 102-8,
    113-14
culture 15-16, 20, 24, 34,
    36-47, 52-3, 68, 71, 76-7,
    102, 106, 112-13, 118,
    120, 135-7, 140; *see also*
    cultural mandate
Cunningham, Merce 4

David 46-9, 67, 69, 79-80,
    82, 90-1
Debussy, Claude Achille
    94-5, 136
Diderot, Denis 68, 137
Durkheim, Emile 41
Dylan, Bob 9, 74, 116, 136

143

electronic music   97
Ellington, 'Duke'   5
Eskimo music   59
ethnomusicology   15, 19,
    137
Evans, Bill   128-9

formalism   53-6, 73
Franklin, Aretha   20

Garner, Erroll   130-1
Gauguin, Paul   95
Goodman, Benny   58-9
Gregorian chant   31-2, 61
Griffith, D. W.   4

Henry, Pierre   8
hymnody   1, 109, 120, 140

Indian music   60-1
IRCAM Centre   43

Jacob, Max   6
Jacques-Dalcroze, Emile
    110, 140
Jagger, Mick   9
James, William   17-18
jazz   13-14, 21, 58, 77,
    80-1, 113, 128-31, 137,
    139-40
John, Elton   9
Jones, Edward   83-4
Jubal   ch. 2 *passim*

Kline, Meredith   40-1,
    135-6
Kodály, Zoltán   110

Lang, Jack   12
Lang, Paul Henry   20, 134

Langer, Susanne K.   70,
    136
L'Engle, Madeleine   102,
    140
Lewis, C. S.   132, 141
Luther, Martin   115

Machaut, Guillaume de
    118
Madonna   89, 139
Malm, Krister   18-19, 134
Malraux, André   98, 140
Manilow, Barry   17, 134
Mattheson, Johann   72
McCartney, Paul   9
Melis, Laszlo   123
Messiaen, Olivier   123-5
Meyer, Leonard B.   66-7,
    137
Mitchell, Tony   3
Monteux, Pierre   16
Murphy, Jeanette Robinson
    131
music: boundaries   4, 6,
    45-51, 64; communication
    118-21; definition   4,
    44-5; education   109-11;
    egalitarian   21, 93-8;
    emotion   54-5, 64-72,
    138; entertainment
    111-14; gift of God   23,
    34, 104, 106, 108; good
    and evil in   93-100; in
    the home   108-9; and
    language   58-64;
    manipulation   86-90;
    meaning   ch. 3 *passim*;
    the media   13-19, 31,
    111; as metaphor   70-8,
    83, 88-90, 98-9; omni-
    presence   5-8, 19, 80;

origins   24-33; pluralism
15-16; power of   9-13,
ch. 4 *passim*; sacred and
secular   47-51; style   11,
75, 102, 116-28; sub-
stance   88; trance with
86-9, 138; *see also* Arabic
music; Bible and music;
black American music;
blues; calling; electronic
music; Eskimo music;
hymnody; jazz; Rhythm
and Blues; rock and roll;
Tonga music; West
African music
'Muzak'   12, 50
Myers, Rollo   6

naturalism   30-1, 68

Oliveros, Paul   97
Orff, Carl   110

Patton, Charley   57-8
Peterson, Oscar   13
Pink Floyd   116
Plato   79, 82-3, 85
Powers, Harold   60-1, 64,
135-7
Prince   85, 99, 138
propaganda art   55-6, 132
psycho-accoustical theory
67, 86, 88-90

Rameau, Jean-Philippe
29-31, 135
Régimbal, Jean-Paul   84-5,
138
Reich, Steve   123
Rhythm and Blues   84
rock   *see* rock and roll

rock and roll   1, 9, 18-20,
84-6, 89-90, 98-9, 116-17;
see also video-clips
Rookmaaker, Hans   81,
137, 139
Rouget, Gilbert   86-9, 139
Rousseau, Jean-Jacques   30,
135
Russolo, Luigi   7, 134

Satie, Erik   6
Schaeffer, Francis   119-20,
140
Schnabel, Arthur   14
Schönberg, Arnold   20-1,
121-2
serial music   53-62
Shostakovich   10
silence   7
Simon, Carly   3
Soviet Union   10-11, 58-9,
80-1
Stein, Jeff   3
Stockhausen, Karlheinz   8,
73, 96-7
Stokowski, Leopold   16
Stravinsky, Igor   54-5, 61-2,
118-19, 126-8, 136
structuralism   53, 73
Stryper   117
style   *see* music: style
Szemzo, Tibor   123

Thomas, Theodore   112-13
Tonga music   120-1, 140

Verdi, Giuseppe   119
video-clip   3-5, 20
Voodoo music   87

Wagner, Richard   4

Wallis, Roger   18, 134
Ward, James   117
Watts, Isaac   63, 81
Webern, Anton von   20-1,
  95-6, 134, 139-40
West African music   19,
  131

Westminster Confession of
  Faith   114
Williams, John   71

Zwingli, Huldrich   115